My Life as I Have Lived It

The Autobiography
of
Rosina Corrothers-Tucker

(1881–1987)

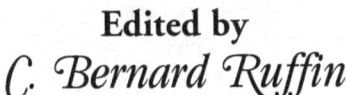

Edited by
C. Bernard Ruffin

HERITAGE BOOKS
2011

HERITAGE BOOKS
AN IMPRINT OF HERITAGE BOOKS, INC.

Books, CDs, and more—Worldwide

For our listing of thousands of titles see our website at
www.HeritageBooks.com

Published 2011 by
HERITAGE BOOKS, INC.
Publishing Division
100 Railroad Ave. #104
Westminster, Maryland 21157

Copyright © 2011 C. Bernard Ruffin

Other books by the author:

*Kemp, Sparrow and Greenwood Families of Norfolk, Virginia:
Their Ancestors and Descendants*

Norfolk, Virginia Registry of Free Negroes, 1835–1861, Abstracts

All rights reserved. No part of this book may be reproduced or transmitted in any form or by any means, electronic or mechanical, including photocopying, recording or by any information storage and retrieval system without written permission from the author, except for the inclusion of brief quotations in a review.

International Standard Book Numbers
Paperbound: 978-0-7884-5364-9
Clothbound: 978-0-7884-8919-8

Introduction

On the evening of my sixteenth birthday I reluctantly accompanied my Aunt Louise to a bazaar at the Fifteenth Street Presbyterian Church, where my family and I were members. The only subject of conversation that evening was the assassination of President Kennedy, which had occurred that afternoon. At some point, there was some sort of program, which I remember only because of a venerable lady who rose to address the people who were gathered there, prefacing her remarks by stating that she was 82 years old. I have no remembrance about what she was talking about—presumably the assassination and the expected consequences—but there was something about this tall, stately brown-skinned, white-haired lady that made a tremendous impression on me.

Not long afterwards I asked my father who this "Mrs. Tucker" was. He immediately identified her as one of the "pillars of the church"(even when he was a boy in the 1920s), a member of one of the most distinguished Negro (that was the term) families in Washington, and the mother of "Big Hank" Corrothers, a college football coach who, though long dead, was still well and fondly remembered at the time.

I had always been fascinated by history and made that subject my major when I went away to Bowdoin College. When I was attending Yale Divinity School I commenced to write the biography of Fanny Crosby, the nineteenth century and early twentieth century poet and hymn-writer, and, in the course of research, interviewed a number of elderly people who had known her. Involved in genealogical research from my teens, I had already conducted extensive interviews of my surviving aunts. After my graduation from Yale, while I was engaged in a long and difficult search for an assignment as a pastor in the Lutheran Church in America, of which I was now a member, the idea came to me that Mrs. Tucker would be an interesting subject of an interview.

On April 29, 1974, I entered in my diary: "I called Mrs. Tucker about an appointment to tape-record her reminiscences. She said many people are after her for that, including reporters from the *Star* [newspaper], so I am to call her next week. On May 6, I noted: "I called Mrs. Tucker, who now is sort of enthusiastic about my tape-recording her reminiscences. She seems to want me to assist her in writing her autobiography. An awesome responsibility!"

I soon learned that Mrs. Tucker was one of the organizers of the Brotherhood of Sleeping Car Porters, the first successful labor union created by and for people of

African descent. A. Philip Randolph, President of the Brotherhood for most of the years of its existence, answered a letter I addressed to him at the behest of Mrs. Tucker that she was indeed one of the most important founders of the union and her contributions were "as important as any man" in making the Brotherhood a success.

From May to December, 1974, with a cassette tape recorder in hand, I met with Mrs. Tucker 17 times at the gracious two story red brick row house near Gallaudet University, which had been her home for nearly six decades. I asked her questions about different subjects, and allowed her to diverge onto other topics as she saw fit. My aunt, Dr. Louise Jones Hubbard, who was head of the French Department at D.C. Teachers' College, graciously offered to transcribe the tapes, which she did. At that point, I would organize the material logically and chronologically, and gave it to Mrs. Tucker to revise as she chose.

The following are some observations I recorded in my diary:

May 15, 1974: "I got the tape recorder from Weezie [my aunt] and went to Mrs. Tucker's on 7th St NE, where I had a rather productive session...Her recollections are rambling, however..."

May 17, 1974: "At 10:30 [AM] I went to Mrs. Tucker's. We had a long session. She discussed her life through her high school days, and gave a moving account of her conversion in 1894 and of her personal faith in Christ at the present time. She bade me write to a B.F. McLaurin for an account from him of her work with the Brotherhood. She also wants a statement from A. Philip Randolph..."

May 27: "I went to Mrs. Tucker. Somehow I was already weary and somehow not as animated as I should have been. I didn't know just how to organise Mrs. Tucker's divers memories into an orderly pattern today, as she talked about her work of organising the Brotherhood of Pullman Porters. I never knew what a Pullman porter was until today. I thought it was a redcap."

June 3: "I had a taping session with Mrs. Tucker. She, among other things, reminisced, off the record, about her second husband Berthea J. Tucker; she said at first she was upset that he spent so much time away from home (or rr runs) but then, when he did come home, she came to be sorry that he wasn't away more of the time; she said he was introverted and impossible to know; said he had a 'deep, deep inferiority complex.' She wants me to return when I have some of the transcripts typed up.

June 7: "I went to Weezie's. She has finished transcribing (by hand) all seven tapes of Mrs. Tucker—a phenomenal job."

October 30: "I went to Mrs. Tucker's. She...told about her evil 2nd husband and how she separated from him for about three years...

Mrs. Tucker wrote in a preface to her work:"When I retired from my post of the International Secretary-Treasurer of the Ladies' Auxiliary of the Brotherhood of Sleeping Car Porters (BSCP) a labor organization, Brother B. F. McLaurin, the International Eastern Zone Supervisor, suggested, in fact, insisted, that I write a memoir of my activities especially covering the BSCP, but I simply had not the confidence to get started with it until a few years later when Rev. Bernard Ruffin, a former student in my Sunday School[1] who had graduated from college for a career in the Christian ministry, called on me for an interview relative to what Washington, D.C. was like when I was young. After the interview, he read several of my prepared speeches which he termed 'real sermons.'"

A rough draft of the manuscript was ready early in 1975, and for some months we worked at it to try to get into a form in which it would be accepted by publishers. In fact, during the next year or so, I sent Mrs. Tucker's autobiography to a number of publishers, only to receive rejection slips.

---

[1] This is true only generally; Mrs. Tucker was one of the supervisors of the Sunday School at Fifteenth Street, but she was never my teacher.

In researching her family, I discovered that Mrs. Tucker and I were almost certainly related, at least distantly. Her great-grandfather, Harry Ruffin was born in King and Queen County, Virginia in or around 1800; my second great grandfather, Ottaway F. Ruffin, Jr., was born in the same county in 1814. She was delighted when I asked her if I could address her as "Cousin Rose" and for a couple of years I received Christmas cards from her addressed that way.

In the late 1970s, however, I got a rather curt note from "Mrs. Rosina C. Tucker" demanding that I return to her all five copies of the manuscript "at once." She was a kind, good-hearted person who could be gentle, but there were times when she expressed her dissatisfaction in no uncertain terms. "I don't allow anybody to walk over me," she once told a reporter. "I have learned to fight with words. I don't cuss."[2] I sent her all five manuscripts, as she desired, and, for sometime her attitude toward me was one of decided coolness. I have never discovered the reason, and assumed that one of her friends had convinced her that I was taking advantage of her for mercenary reasons. However, her attitude at the time might be explained by her statement in her preface: "When I read the initial transcribed typed sheets, I doubted that they reflect a clear portrait of me." I had,

---

[2] *Washington Post,* May 26, 1982

indeed, tried to put the final manuscript together in such a way as to make it attractive to publishers, and the version I prepared was perhaps too heavily "ghost-written."

During the next year or so, Mrs. Tucker, with the help of Miss Bettie Plummer and Mrs. Loree Murray, worked on the manuscript, adding material to some of the chapters and revising others.

When, shortly after her hundredth birthday, Mrs. Tucker became a celebrity, traveling to churches, schools and other audiences all over the United States, to tell her story, and even appearing on television talk shows, she frequently quoted from her autobiography, and, when she died, I assumed that it had been completed. The years went by and Rosina Corrothers-Tucker's autobiography never saw the light of day.

Over a period of years, I made inquiries of several people who were close to Mrs. Tucker. Nobody knew what had become of the manuscript. Mrs. Tucker's niece, her only surviving relative, was quite brusque, and said, "Well, you never could get it published when she was alive, so why are you interested in it now?" After my retirement from teaching history in the public schools in 2008, I intensified my efforts. I obtained a copy of Mrs. Tucker's will, and learned that she left most of her estate to the "to the Leadership Conference on Civil Rights in memory of my happy days working with its leaders, A. Philip Randolph and their fellow workers." I contacted the Leadership Conference, only to learn that they did not possess the Tucker papers, but informed me that Melinda Chateauvert, a professor at the University of Maryland, had used them in writing the book *Marching Together: The Women of the Brotherhood of Sleeping Car Porters*. Contacting Dr. Chateauvert, I learned, to my relief, that the Tucker papers had been given to her. She graciously sent me a CD of the autobiography in her possession, and I learned that Mrs. Tucker had apparently never finished it after all. She had left intact some portions of the manuscripts I had prepared, revised others, but left several large gaps in her life story and left some chapters incomplete or unfinished.

Although I returned what I had considered the finished, or near-finished manuscript, I retained the tapes, the transcripts made by my aunt, as well as the first and second draft of much of the work. Working with the material preserved by Dr. Chateauvert as well as the material already in my possession, I have been able to complete the autobiography, in such a way as would (hopefully) be pleasing to Mrs. Tucker, and fulfilling what I consider a sacred trust to her to make her story known.

The portions that Mrs. Tucker revised, I have generally left as they were. The gaps in her narrative I filled with the material that I had. Some of the chapters that she prepared, that were mostly lists of people she helped or who helped her, or that consisted of testimonies and tributes, I placed in appendices after the main text of the book, and arranged the material in a general chronological order, and my hope is that the story of a truly remarkable individual may be known to succeeding generations.

Acknowledgments

I thank Brother Benjamin F. McLaurin for urging me to write of myself because it added purpose to my life; also I thank him for refreshing my memory to some specific events relating to the union and for his constant inquiries as to my progress with it.

Many thanks are due Rev. Bernard Ruffin for his interest and for obtaining the vital statistics regarding my great grandparents and for his ever readiness to give me his moral support throughout the four years it took me to complete this effort.

Many thanks are due to Miss Bettie Plummer, not only for typing the first chapters of this book, but for her interest in the subject matter. She often remarked that she could not type my script for reading it. This was very encouraging to me. Also she conversed with some members of the faculty of Howard University and others about me, stressing my age, which at that time was 95 years, and because of her, a member of the faculty in the History Department at Howard U. called me to congratulate me, saying that there is a need for Black writers to write about Black people because every scrap of history is important now and will be more so in the future. I was grateful for his call.

I was very sorry to lose Miss Plummer as my typist, but I was very happy when I learned of her appointment to the Department of Political Science and History of the University of Arkansas, at Pine Bluff.

I am grateful to my neighbor, Mrs. Loree Murray, who on hearing of my losing my typist, Miss Plummer, volunteered to complete the typing of the remaining chapters. It was quite a sacrifice for her, because she is a homemaker with a husband and seven children and has a government job. During this period I became critically ill with a heart ailment and could not write for over ten months; it was then she took care of many of my needs after the nurse left for the day. She spent nights with me and when she could not be with me, she would send one of her children in case of emergency. There are other persons I am thankful for, some of whom I have written of in the body of the book.

The Author [Rosina Corrothers-Tucker]

This book is dedicated to and in remembrance of my son, Henry Harvey Corrothers, better affectionately known to the public in general as "Hank" Corrothers, for his supreme love for and devotion to me and his responsiveness to the needs of many students under his instruction, and to people generally.

Prologue

For many years my friends have been urging me to write my autobiography. When the suggestion was first made to me, I was incredulous, for I had never believed that there was anything extraordinary about my life. However, since I have lived so long and since there is no denying that my experiences have been many and varied, I set down my story in hopes that some of the younger generation might learn from my joys and sorrows, successes and failures, triumphs and tragedies. The most striking thing about my life is that it seems to me that I have had so little control of my destiny. Those things which I have done I more or less happened into by force of circumstance. It seems that at many points in my life, I have been forced by an unseen Hand to do what I have done. That Power which has propelled me throughout the course of my life I can identify only with God.

Chapter One: From Slavery to Freedom

In 1865, the year the Civil War ended, there came to Washington, DC, up from King and Queen County, Virginia, a shoemaker by the name of Henry Ruffin."Harry" Ruffin, as he was known, was a coal-black man, then 65 years old, but still strong and vigorous.[3] Until then he had been a slave, but even though he first knew freedom at this advanced age, he was eager to make a new life for himself and his family. Finding a place to live was the problem. Most dwellings in Washington had large long back yards which opened onto alleys. In some of these alleys were stables where the well-to-do owners kept their horses and carriages. There were carpenter shops, blacksmith shops, furniture repair and upholstery shops, and other small businesses. Noting the influx of these newly freed people, white speculators were quick to build rows of shacks and shanties in these alleys throughout the city. In them were no modern sanitary facilities, but water and toilets were on the outside. It was into one of these shanties in the alley between 6th and 7th and

---

[3] My own Ruffin ancestors also lived in King and Queen County, Virginia, in the early 1800s. My patrilinear Y-chromosome DNA traces back not to Africa, but rather India, so if Rosina Tucker was related, as she probably was, through the King and Queen Ruffins, her great-grandfather Harry had at least one ancestor who originated in India.

L & M Streets, N.W., now called 6½ Street[4], that Harry Ruffin, my great-grandfather, the head of the clan, crowded his large family.

With him he had his wife, the former Mildred Turner, affectionately known as "Millie." She was 69. With them came their 37 year old daughter, Mary Ann, the widow of Alexander Pollard, and three sons: Louis, 31; Henry, Jr., 30, and William, 27. And this was not all. Along with Mary Ann Pollard and her daughter Jane were a cousin, Mary Harvey, and five children of a dead daughter of Harry and Millie Ruffin.: 17 year old Harry Harvey, 15 year old Griffin, 13 year old Lee Roy, nine year old Jeanette, and six year old Katherine, or "Kate." The Harvey children had lost both parents in childhood and were raised by Aunt Mary Ann.

Lee Roy Harvey was my father. I do not know too much about my father's early life, as in those days, people just did not sit down and discuss things. And a child did not dare to ask. You would just have to catch things as you could.. I was always interested in my ancestry, but my interest was not shared by most of my family. Even my older sister would accuse me of "always hunting up old relatives." So I really never learned too much about my

---

[4] It was then called "Goat Alley." Mrs. Tucker did not want to mention the name!

ancestry, but I wish I had, for I understand that some of the Ruffins of Virginia are very well educated and very well-to-do. I have always wanted to go to my father's birthplace and make myself known to my distant cousins, but have never had the opportunity to do so.

Harvey, of course, was not my father's real name. There is no way now of ascertaining what it is. When the Africans were brought here as slaves, they were given the names of their owners. My father's family was no exception. So the name Harvey is really the "white folks" name and not our own. I can see why so many of the young people of our race to-day are using African names: so that they can have a name they can call their own.

The family of Harry Ruffin crowded themselves into the small house and sought out successfully a means of livelihood. Harry set up shop with his son William and there in the home began to make as well as repair shoes for customers both black and white. Louis worked as a blacksmith and young Henry obtained a position as a messenger in the federal government. It was not long until the family was able to purchase a frame house at 623 L Street, around the corner from where they first lived. Here great-grandfather Henry and wife Millie lived with Aunt Mary Ann until their deaths. Louis and Henry Ruffin established homes of their own, and William apparently died at an early age.

I have fond memories of Aunt Mary Ann[5]. She was fair in complexion and was a lovely person—very kind and motherly. Her daughter Jane lived with her. Jane later married a man named Blount, whose first name I do not remember, and there were two sons, Louis Charles and Frederick. Louis, the elder[6], became a brilliant young man who established the Great Lakes Insurance Company in Detroit, Michigan. Frederick was a very handsome youngster who died when he was 14 years old. His death almost broke Cousin Jane's heart.

My early childhood was spent in the heart of a very close family circle and my earliest recollections are of my relatives. I was born November 4, 1881 at 1011 4th Street, N.W., in a five room frame house that has long since been demolished. All Papa's relatives lived close by. Aunty Jeanette and Aunty Kate lived across the street from us. Just a block or so away, at 623 L Street, lived Papa's grandparents, along with his Aunt Mary Ann Pollard. I have but a vague recollection of my great-grandfather, Harry

---

[5] Mary Ann Ruffin Pollard (1828-1912)

[6] Louis Charles Blount (1892-1967)

Ruffin, who died at the age of 97[7] but I remember Great Grandmother Ruffin well, for she lived until I was in my early teens, when she was 102.[8] I can still remember going upstairs to the room where the little old lady, very fair in complexion, with an old fashioned lace kerchief on her silvery head and shawl on her shoulders, sat in a rocking chair. I remember how Papa delighted in talking with her and how she thought that there were none like us, his children. My sisterNettie and I visited her and Aunt Mary almost every Sunday.

Not far away, between 4th and 5th and G and H Streets was a short street called Washington Street, where my father's uncle, Henry Ruffin, lived with his wife Eliza. Their daughter Ellen was a woman of exceptional beauty, so much that, as young as I was, I observed that even while sitting in church, her husband could not keep his eyes from off her.

I have vivid memories of my father's uncle, Louis Ruffin, who later lived at 1816 Vermont Avenue. He was a slight erect man with good features and his skin coloring was quite black. At that time he had quit blacksmithing and had purchased a hansom cab and gone into business for himself.

---

[7] According to his death certificate, Harry Ruffin was 89 when he died in 1889. Mildred was 101 when she died in 1897.

He often visited Aunt Jeanette at her place of business and how I thought him to be the "grandest" person ever, with his long black coachman's coat with two rows of big brass buttons down the front; his beaver top hat; his refinement and business demeanor made an undying impression on my childish mind. He could not read or write, so, at times, he would ask his nephew Louis Blount, Jane's son, to read the society column for important events sponsored by very important people and organizations. He would be there at the end of the affairs, for he knew he would be hailed to take a distinguished person to his home. He also knew routine times his services would be needed. This is how he earned his living and he did very well at it. Uncle Louis was very religious. He was a deacon in the Mount Carmel Baptist Church, which at the time was located at 4th and L Streets, N.W., right at the corner of where my family lived. I was visiting Great Grandma Millie one Sunday afternoon when Uncle Louis brought the Elements and serve his mother Communion. Though a very young child then, I have never forgotten that beautiful scene—Great Grandmother being served Communion by her son.

Papa's brothers and sisters also lived nearby. Uncle Harry Harvey[9] bought a house on 5th Street, N.W., between P

---

[9] Henry "Harry" Harvey (c.1848-1885) married Maria Macon on July 26, 1875, in Washington.

and Q. He worked in the Patent Office. He died in his late 30s and his only son Lawrence[10] came to live with Aunt Jeanette and Aunt Kate. Aunt Jeanette was a very good cook and she opened what was called in that period an "eating house." She was one of the kindest persons I have ever known. Not only did she take in Lawrence, her dead brother Harry's son, but when her brother Griffin died[11] leaving two orphans, Sidney and Eva, she took Sidney[12] into her home, while Eva went to live with her maternal grandmother. When Eva was a teenager, her grandmother died, and Aunt Jeanette took her into her home to live and cared for her through high school and teachers' college, until she obtained a position as a teacher in the public schools. Eva married a lawyer by the name of Blake, at which time she was an English teacher at the Martha Murray Washington High School. In her later years, Aunt Jeanette[13] married Samuel

---

[10] Both Harry Harvey and his son Lawrence Harvey (1878-1895) died of tuberculosis. Harry's wife Maria seems to have died shortly after her husband.

[11] Griffin Harvey (c.1850-1881) married Virginia Baylor October 26, 1871. He died of an "abscess of the pelvis" at Freedmen's Hospital. Mrs. Tucker believed that his wife Virginia died in a fire.

[12] Mrs. Tucker believed that Sidney was handicapped.

[13] Jeanette Harvey Turner (c.1856-1915) lived at 309 K Street, N.W. in the 1890s and was described as a "confectioner" in the DC City Directory.

Turner [in 1903] and cousin Mary[14], a seamstress, married a Baptist minister by the name of Luke Best [in 1900].

My father, Lee Roy Harvey, was born in King and Queen County, Virginia in December, 1851. He stood about 5'6" tall and was of medium build. Of fair complexion, he had black hair and a few freckles around his nose. After he came to Washington, apprenticed to his grandfather, he went to night school, to learn to read and write, a luxury that neither his grandparents nor his aunts and uncles were ever able to afford. He also took music lessons and became proficient on the organ and piano. When he was in his twenties, he met and fell in love with Henrietta Mills, a girl who was living in service at 921 G Street, N.W. They were married in April, 1873. Henrietta, my mother, was born in Fairfax County, Virginia. She was "just a little missy when Richmond fell," her mother, Grandma Caroline Thompson, often stated.[15] Mom was separated from her parents and two sisters after the Civil War, when she came to Washington.

---

[14] Mary Harvey (b. circa 1859)

[15] The U.S. Census of 1870 gives her place of birth as "Virginia", but according to the censuses of 1900 1910, and 1920, she was a native of "Maryland." Her age was given as 25 in 1870, making for a birth year of 1845. In each ensuing census she made herself younger. According to the censuses of 1880 and 1900, she would have been born in or around 1852; but in 1910 and 1920, her birth year would have been around 1860. (She seems to have been missed in the census of 1930).

For many years she had no contact whatsoever with them. Mom was only about five feet tall, was plump, small-boned, and brown-skinned with long, nearly straight hair. They used to call it "Madagascar hair."

In time, there were nine children born to them: Roberta Ann, who was born and died in January, 1874; Marietta Lela, born April, 1875; Benjamin Turner, born November, 1877; James Henry, who died at eight months in October, 1880; Rosina Bud, born November 4, 1881; Jeanette Caroline, born November, 1883; Harry Augustus, born July, 1886; Lee Roy Graham, born January, 1889; and Corinne, born July, 1891.

I really have few recollections of my elders talking about slavery. First of all, the Harveys and the Ruffins seemed very reticent about speaking about it in the first place, and, secondly, in those days, children were to be "seen and not heard", and questions on our part were simply taboo. All that I learned came from scraps of conversations of my parents and aunts and uncles and chance remarks that they may have made to others. The only thing that I ever heard Papa say about his childhood was that when he was a boy, he had to sleep on chairs or wherever he happened to be when he was sleepy. He mentioned this only in the context of telling us how he resolved when he was a boy that when he grew into manhood and had children that when they became sleepy, they could go to bed instead of sitting around sleeping, as he had to do so many times.

Many people do not realize that many of the slaves were excellent artisans and craftsmen. Not all slaves simply tilled the soil. Many were skilled workers who in large measure carried on the economy and business of the Old South. Many of the slaves were expert dressmakers. They made the elaborate dresses with the ruffles and laces and tucks and pleats that women wore at that time

If I today have anything of determination and self-reliance; if today I have anything of an unswerving devotion to what I believe is right, such qualities come from my father. He was a man of lofty principle and strong character; but he was a stern Victorian father, however, and very much of an authoritarian. If, on the other hand, I have anything of gentleness, kindness, patience and understanding, these qualities I derive from my mother, for she was a serene imperturbable woman of great religious faith, totally devoted to her children and husband and worthy of emulation.

Papa had learned his trade as a shoemaker from his grandfather. Not only did he repair shoes, but he made them from scratch. His shoes were very popular with wealthy white people. Many times a little girl, I would go into his shop, which was at the time in our home, and watch him wax the threads of a special kind of floss to make it strong, then take a curved awl and make holes both in the upper and lower parts of the sole from the inside, and then turn the shoe inside out and finish with the heels. He made special shoes for people with various orthopedic problems. There were several children in our neighborhood who wore braces and Papa could repair the braces and place the shoes in them. I remember in particular a man in our church who required a heel about six inches in height, due to a disparity in the length of his legs. I have seen Papa add layer of leather until the heel was the desired height.

It was not until my teens that I met Mama's mother, Caroline Mills Thompson (she had remarried after my grandfather's death.)[16] "Aunt Caroline" did have something to say about slavery, and from it I learned that certain slaves were not as hapless and miserable as many others might expect them to have been. It was my grandmother's responsibility to take care of the master's children. She was not a "mammy"—a mammy was a wet nurse. In those days white women were deathly afraid of losing their figure by breast nursing their children so they would delegate the role to one of the slave women, even though it meant that her own children in question were deprived

---

[16] According to census records, Caroline married Henry Thompson, a farmer, around 1878, and had no children by him.

of their sufficient nourishment. Grandmother took care of the older children. Often they were poorly behaved. But she, like all slaves, had ways of handling that. When she got the master's children alone she would severely shake and slap them. "And I just dare you to tell your parents! I just *dare* you!" And they never did! Those children had learned how to "behave" themselves even toward a slave.

I have heard other people say that slaves often resorted to drastic means of avenging themselves on a cruel master. They related instances when slaves would grind up glass and put it in the food of a particularly hated master. Unsuspecting, "Master" would sit down to eat. When he doubled up in pain, the servant who had set before him his fatal meal would sidle up to him and ask solicitously, "Master don't feel so good?" She would continue obsequiously to make over "poor Master" until he died. Since autopsies were rare in that time and place, the white people never suspected otherwise.

Slaves had other means of "beating the system." Most of them were past masters at deceiving white people, and many old slaves I came to know claimed that they could read their masters "like a book." (A peculiar analogy, since most of them could not in fact read). But they had a way of buttering up the white people and getting whatever they wanted from them. When I was in Virginia later in my life, there were still many old former slaves who knew no other livelihood after freedom except getting hand-outs from white people by buttering them up. It was really an art that involved the use of the proper gestures and the right inflections of the voice. I met some old people who would tell a white man, "I was your grandfather's bodyguard" in such a way to get a substantial handout.

Many unpleasant things resulted from slavery, however, that not only were evident at this time, but are still true today to some extent. One of these was an absolute veneration of white people. Although they did not trust them, they held them in idolatrous awe at the same time. I had opportunity to observe this when I was a young pastor's wife in Lexington, Virginia, where our parish was, to a large extent, made up of former slaves and their children. They also had an obsequious veneration of the clergy. There was one old man called "Uncle Jeff", who was pathetic. Whenever the poor old soul approached the lot on which stood our parsonage, he would remove his hat and keep it off until he had cleared the property, a distance of perhaps a hundred yards. His veneration of anyone who happened to be white and that of many of his peers was truly heartrending. Whenever they spoke to anyone who was white, they would remove their hats, even though they did not observe this custom when conversing with members of their own race. Even if they had good cause to believe that something told them by a colored person was right and that told them by a white person was wrong, they would follow the white person's advice, not because they were afraid of any reprisals, but simply because the person giving the advice was white. There are still some colored people today who feel that they have still to bow down to white people. My parents, however, were decidedly not of that school of thought. "Don't believe everything you read in the newspapers," Papa often said.

Chapter II--A Girlhood in Old Washington

Even before I started to school at the old Banneker Building on 3rd Street, N.W., between K and L, Papa had taught me how to read and write, as he taught each of my brothers and sisters at a similar age. He was truly a remarkable man. Although a former slave, he was determined that all of his children would have a good education and obtain good jobs. "I never want any of my girls working in white people's kitchens," he often said. Consequently, he wanted us to receive an excellent intellectual background from an early age. He hung a huge blackboard in our kitchen, which he used to tutor only us, but neighbors' children. Parents with children who had trouble learning at school would send them to Lee Roy Harvey. He would scream and yell and rant and rave like a mad conductor of a symphony orchestra, but he succeeded in instructing even the dullest of pupils.

Papa was a serious man, reading deep books at every opportunity. He loved discussions on subjects of the day, literature and religion and current events. There were four Baptist pastors who made his shop a sort of forum for such discussions. I recollect an instance when one of these pastors, whose name I will not disclose, was very happy to relate that his church had paid of its long-standing debt.

Many pastors had come to the conclusion that as long as their members were in debt and struggling to pay it off, they would not have the time to carry on their accustomed church quarrels.

This minister was inclined to doubt this assertion, and asked my father's opinion. I am sure that Papa's answer favored the congregation's need for a period of rest. I am intrigued as to how some ministers manipulate their congregation's need for a period of rest. I am intrigued as to how some ministers have manipulated their congregations in past years, and I suspect many are doing just that today, but in a more ingenious manner. But, interestingly enough, the person to whom Pop went when he had trouble understanding some passage in the Scripture was his aged grandmother [Mildred] who could not read or write, but had an uncanny ability to interpret it. I remember one particular occasion when Papa was troubled by Our Lord's promise to remain with his followers "even unto the end of the earth," he went to Grandmother Ruffin, who told him it meant "to the end of your life."

Mom had a great interest in our schooling and saw to it that we did our homework. Her chief interests were her husband, whom she faithfully backed up in all his decisions, and her children and her home. We often went with her to do the grocery shopping at the Center Market, which stood on Pennsylvania Avenue, running from 7th to 12th Streets, on the site of the present National Archives Building and Department of Justice. In this market one could get any kind of food one desired, both in the way of meats and vegetables and fruits. Around 11th and 12th Streets I remember they had nothing but chickens, turkeys and geese and such. In those days, one could get a pound of sugar for 4 or 5 cents. But, of course, people were not paid much. School teachers would start at $40 per month. But in those days a young school teacher could dress and "put on airs" and have enough left over to help her parents, too, on that salary.

    We always had plenty to eat. There was a great deal of seafood. In those days, vendors would come around selling fish that were still kicking. We could get six herring for ten cents. We also ate a lot of oysters. And then we had ham, cabbage, potatoes of different kinds, and kale. I never heard of spinach until I was living in New York. And I never heard of collard greens and okra, which became popular with people just up from the South. I refuse to eat okra to this day. We never had chitterlings, either. At church socials, however, they were sold. When we went to a church social, pig feet were also sold as part of the refreshments. What are now called "hot dogs" were simply called smoked sausage. It was not until around 1900 that a newspaperman up in New York named T.A. Dorgan dreamed up the term "hot dog." We did not have hamburgers or anything that fit their description, but we had steaks, roast beef, pork chops, and loin of pork in abundance. I especially loved the way Mom cooked baked beans, in the "southern style." She would boil the beans until they were almost done, then transfer them to the oven. She would place over them a piece of salt pork known as a "streak of lean and a streak of fat." She would slice the skin of this in such a way as to leave little squares on top. As the beans baked, the grease would ooze out of the salt pork and saturate the beans. Oh, how we would just kill ourselves eating them! We sometimes had ice cream, but for desert we mainly ate fruit, especially apples, strawberries and blackberries, as well as pies and cakes—mostly apple and prune pies.

All of our family was musical. My parents could not live without music. Our home always had a piano and an organ, and, as time went on, we accumulated a brass horn, an accordion, a mandolin, a violin, a saxophone, and a clarinet. Papa gave us our earliest music lessons, then sent us to professional teachers. Although he had no formal musical training (that I know of), parents from all over Washington sent their children to him for both lessons on the piano and for singing lessons. Papa had a wonderful baritone voice. He also organized a chorus of men and women who would get together at regular intervals and spend an entire evening singing, merely for the pleasure of it. They sang both light and classical pieces. I especially remember a song which began:

> The wolf is on the hill
>
> We hear him howling still.

I think it must have been some sort of round. Several of the boys and girls he trained became accomplished musicians. Most distinguished was Walter Loving, who was later to organize the Filipino Constabulary Band, which was well-known in the early part of the twentieth century. He always acknowledged his gratitude to my father, and whenever in later years he came to this area from his many travels, he would call on Papa, and together they would sit down and go over musical scores that the band played.

All of us children loved music. There was somebody always playing one of the instruments. Although no one was allowed to touch an instrument after 10 p.m., I often wonder how the neighbors felt, for they surely never had any rest until our curfew. Almost all of us were early proficient in music. I suppose Benny, Harry, and I were the best musicians. Benny mastered the violin and taught that instrument to the rest of us. He later became the Chief Musician in the 48th Infantry Band in the U.S. Army, where he played the clarinet. Harry was one of the first colored people to learn to play the saxophone. Marietta learned slowly, but eventually became an excellent organist. In 1889, when I was seven, she, then fourteen, became the organist at the John Wesley Methodist Church, then located on Connecticut Avenue, directly opposite DeSales Street, a position she held for many years.. But it was not long before I was substituting for her on her vacations. Nettie could play the piano a little, but she did not seek to make a profession of it. Nevertheless, she loved music and when she grew up and married, she bought a player piano and was the first of us to purchase a crystal radio set and as radio sets developed and improved, she would get one. Television sets were not on the market during her lifetime, but if they had been, she would have had one in her home.

Marietta was always irked that her younger sister Rose could play the piano better than she could, and this was perhaps the cause of some friction between us which rose at a fairly early age. Things were not helped any by Aunt Jeanette, who convinced Papa that we younger children should not address Marietta familiarly, but rather, call her "Sister." Consequently, "Sister" was made at a very early age a sort of assistant mother to the rest of us. As a result, she became quite bossy and we often resented her.

However, we could not express our resentment in any open way. Ours was a very strict household. Papa was a typical Victorian father, stern, authoritarian, and often frankly terrifying Like most of his contemporaries, he insisted on absolute obedience. (I have sometimes wondered whether this was a carryover from slavery.). Few fathers and mothers in those days ever displayed much open affection for their children, and he was no exception. Parents feared "spoiling" them. Papa never displayed his great love for us or his great pride in us when we were children. Later I came to resent this, but, at that time, my only reaction was awe. I do not think that he was justified in some of the things he did. Often we got a slap or whipping without understanding what it was for. Whatever a teacher said about us he believed without question and our word counted for nothing. Often Papa punished us for things that were not really our fault. For instance, in those days there was no running water in most Washington homes, but we had running water in our back yards. To get a drink of cool water, parents would send their children for spring water, which could be obtained from the iron pumps that stood on many street corners. We had to lug large crockery pitchers filled with water. Those pitchers were for the water to be used in the bedroom for baths, for there was no indoor plumbing in those days, and baths were taken in large wash tubs. At any rate, because the pitchers were crockery, when a child was sent to the pump for water, oftentimes he or she returned with the pitcher chipped or broken. It was just hard for a child to avoid breaking the pitcher once in a while. I remember times when I was excessively punished by Papa for accidents connected with this chore. The pitchers were so easy to break! Sometimes I think if we had only been given a tin pail, it would have been better, but then, these cost quite a bit of money, and my parents were not well-to-do. But not only did we get frequent slaps and whippings for we knew not what, we were afraid to ask questions.

Papa taught us never to be afraid. One day, when we were little, Nettie and I were standing at the window when we saw what we thought was a horrible goblin. Papa saw our fear and called the "goblin" over and showed us that it was simply a child with a false face [i.e. a mask]. We were not allowed to be afraid of anything.

We had a simple sheltered life. Mom and Papa, like many of their friends, were not fully aware of national or world affairs as people tend to be today. Their life was their church, their family and their neighborhood. We all had certain chores to do. I had to help Mom with the breakfast. Marietta had to do the cleaning. The boys took care of the fires and ashes. Nettie went across the street to help my Aunt Jeanette at her eating house. Aunt Jeanette's was a small dining room with just a few tables. Students at Howard University would board with her. She was an excellent cook and I still remember to this day the pies and cakes that she made. At any rate, Nettie was sent to help her in her dining room in the morning before school and after.

Music was our chief recreation. But there were others. Sunday afternoons, after church, were devoted to some kind of family recreation. We would often walk to the Pension Office Park at 4th and G Streets, N.W. where we would enjoy the beautiful trees and shrubbery and flowers. We would go to visit my parents' friends, the Edwards, who lived near Gallaudet College, the institution for the deaf at the corner from where I now live. In those days it was surrounded by a high stone wall and we would refer to it as "The Crazy House." All through there were woods and vacant space. They used to have cows out there and sell milk. There was a little creek that flowed through the area. One day one of the Edwards boys fell into it and drowned.

We would also walk to the Potomac and Ohio Railroad Depot at 6th and B Sts, N.W., the site of the present National Gallery of Art. We boarded our train here when we went to our Sunday School picnics in rural Bladensburg, Maryland. But some Sunday afternoons we just walked there for recreation. It was a dull, dark, dingy place with ugly dark wooden benches. There was a plaque on the wall to designate this building as the site of the assassination of President Garfield, which occurred the year I was born.

There was a gold star on the floor to mark the exact spot where he fell.

When I was a little older and in high school, my two friends, Sadie Shorter and Hattie Collier went to the Smithsonian Institution. Here there were stuffed animals and birds and dinosaur skeletons. But I remember most vividly the Medical Museum with hideous reproductions of the effects of various maladies and gruesome specimens of limbs and organs affected by various diseases. What I remember most vividly is seeing a coal miner's lung in a glass urn. It was absolutely black. I can remember that as vividly as if it was only yesterday that I saw it. At a very early age I was struck by the hardships under which many of our working men have had to toil.

In those days, there was a trolley route called the Belt Line, which went right by our home. I do not now remember the exact route it took, but it did go through 11th Street, N.W. Many of the people who worked at the "Bureau" (of Engraving), took this car, so evidently it went by the Bureau, at 14th and B Streets, S.W. Sunday many parents put their children on this car and they would go all around the city and back alone. In those days one did not have to worry about being kidnaped or molested and they got a scenic tour of the city.

Washington was beautiful. All government grounds were full of beautiful flowers and there were green parks everywhere. Most streets were dominated by gigantic elms, which met to form a leafy canopy. There was very little crime. I could walk late at night from Connecticut and L, where there was church where I sometimes served as organist, to 1st and K Streets, where I was living, completely without fear and also without encountering a single conveyance. Horses and carriages were used mostly in business districts, and the streets were cleaned of horse filth every night.

Wednesday evenings around 5:30 we went to the Capitol and Saturday afternoons to the Monument Grounds to hear John Philip Sousa conduct the Marine Band. I can still see Sousa conducting. He had a round face, and, as I remember him, was not too tall and rather stout. He played all kinds of music, especially his marches, for he was known as the "March King." We used to buy his marches in sheet music form and play them at home on our piano.

Christmas was not the production it is today. Maybe we had Santa Claus, but we did not get a lot of extra things. I never remember getting much at all. We never had a Christmas tree in those days, for that did not become the custom in Washington until much later. But Mom would make cakes which we ate along with lemonade. And Papa all through the year would make five gallons of root beer at a time in a big boiler and bottle it so that we could drink it whenever we wanted to. He would also get a demijohn of New Orleans Molasses so we could make taffy as well as eat it over our pancakes.

I remember some awful snows when I was a child. I was always very sensitive to cold weather and did not like to go out in it. I preferred studying. But my brothers had sleds and sometimes they and their friends made toboggans and went down the hilly streets in them. Summers were excruciatingly hot. It got so hot upstairs that Mom would make pallets on the floor of the living room so that we could sleep there to obtain some partial relief.

I have never known what it is to live in a segregated neighborhood. Where we lived, on 4th Street, between K and L, N.W. was well integrated. On a given block one would find a white family, then two colored families, then maybe two white families, and one colored. Although I do not remember my parents having any especially close friends who were white, we got along and there was little trouble. I remember my brother Benny beating up a white boy for calling us "nigger" and he and his friends grabbing and pulling the hair of "tow-heads" as we called the white boys, but, by and large, relations were very good. Colored people lived all over. I remember no restrictions to certain areas of the city. Race relations were good at that time and remained good until the time of Woodrow Wilson.

Segregation became bad after President Wilson came in.[17] I understand that his wife's attitude caused a great deal of dissatisfaction among the race. I understand that she wanted to segregate the street cars, but that didn't happen. But, with Wilson, segregation was in the air, it was in the people.

There were some congressmen who dependent on their constituency to put them in Congress, because of their people's hatred for Negroes, would pretend to be prejudiced, even if they weren't.. They got back into Congress term after term by degrading the Negro. Ben Tillman[18] was a rabid Negro hater and every time he'd make a speech, it would be against the Negro. Eventually he had a stroke of paralysis, and he came back to Congress and was able to function to some extent, but he said, "Don't let the niggers start praying for you. Just don't let those niggers start praying for you." He meant that his incapacitation was a result of the prayers of the Negroes. He never got over the stroke and died shortly afterwards.

---

[17] Woodrow Wilson was President between 1913 and 1921.

[18] Benjamin Ryan Tillman (1847-1918), U.S. Senator from South Carolina from 1895 to 1918.

I remember but one area of the city where a black would be given a hard time, and that was Swampoodle, which was the area around the Roman Catholic Church of St. Aloysius Gonzaga on North Capitol Street, around H and I Streets. This area was inhabited by Irish immigrants who were known to take out after strange Negroes who happened through their sections. One of the Edwards boys took music lessons from Papa and had to walk from Northeast through Swampoodle to get to our house. Often he had to run to escape these gangs of furious Irishmen. On one occasion I heard him tell Pop that, "I ran so fast through the puddles that my feet didn't get wet!" But, unlike many cities in those days, we could board the trolleys where and when we wanted, and could sit in any part of them. The schools were segregated and I do not believe colored people could go to most of the restaurants downtown. But there were colored men who ran some very fine restaurants. In fact, some of these, although run by Negroes, catered to white only. I remember one such restaurant on Pennsylvania Avenue which was run by a man named Wormley[19]. But people did not go to restaurants much in those days, anyway, so it was not a terrific problem. If the theaters were segregated, that

---

[19] James Wormley ran an upscale restaurant at 15th and H Streets, N.W., near Pennsylvania Avenue. Although he died in 1884, when Mrs. Tucker was 3, his son continued to operate the establishment well into the 1890s.

posed no problem whatsoever for us, for Mom and Pop were staunch Baptists from the old school who were dead-set against theater-going of any kind.

The Washington I grew up in, which then had a population of fewer than 300,000, was a very agreeable place, virtually free of slums and relatively free of crime. All up 14th Street, even around the vicinity of T and U Streets, where for many years there have been terrible slums, there were when I was a girl fine residences. It was not until later that businessmen turned the lower levels of these homes into shops. Both colored and white lived in this area, as was the case in most other areas of the city, such as Georgetown, Capitol Hill, and Foggy Bottom. Where the main building of the Library of Congress now stands there were some very good homes. They were slightly below the level of the street. Foggy Bottom, where the State Department and the Watergate Hotel complex now are was then a mixed residential area. On 19th and E, I believe, there lived the Burrell family. Later into that family was born the famous scientist, Charles Drew[20], the grandson who devised a way of storing blood plasma during World War II. Very poor people lived in the alleys, and some in sections of Southwest.

---

[20] Charles Richard Drew (1904-1950), a prominent Washington physician and medical researcher, developed large-scale blood banks during World War II.

This section, along with Swampoodle, was probably the worst area of the city. When we were kids, my brothers and sisters and I were deadly afraid of Southwest. There was one part of it they called "Hell's Bottom" and another part they called "Bloody Field", and the accounts of the murders I heard in association with it were nearly enough to make my hair stand erect. There was one man in our church named Stewart who was a policeman and had his beat in Southwest. He commanded enormous respect. The mere mention that "Black Diamond" was coming was enough to send loafers, drunks, thieves, and prostitutes scurrying.

There were many fine people who lived in Southwest, however. Many colored people bought property there and started businesses. One such person whom I knew as a child was a man named Jarvis, who became a Baptist preacher, but also owned a restaurant on the wharf. They shucked oysters and clams there. Men went all through the city with their carts, selling oysters and clams, with all kinds of condiments. For in those days, for fast food, one did not go to McDonald's for a hamburger or to Colonel Sanders for fried chicken, but bought hot waffles or raw oysters seasoned with red peppers from street vendors with push carts.

When I was a child, most women wore aprons. I never saw anyone covering the head with a bandanna. Men wore their hair short. It was considered fashionable to part the hair, and many black men, whose hair would not naturally part, would have the barber shave a part in their hair.

There were many people in those days who were very black—absolutely black. There are not as many really black people anymore.

The Italian organ grinder was also a familiar sight on the streets of Washington in those days. After my little sister Corinne was born when I was nine, I used to enjoy carrying her in my arms, following the organ grinder. I always loved music, but more than that, I was attracted to the antics of the monkey and to the dancing that took place. Mom and Papa were against dancing, and, to see the saloon-keeper's daughter dance when the organ grinder stopped before one of the saloons that seemed to be on every corner, was a new experience. After the girl had danced, the monkey would take a cup and gather up the pennies the amused bystanders would toss to him.

There were some more sober experiences in my childhood, too. When I was very little, Papa went to work at the Government Printing Office. Shortly after that, he had an accident, and I remember him lying in a darkened room, very, very sick. After that, he went back to his shoe business. Papa developed a "plug of blood" (blood clot) in his hip, where he had been kicked by a horse when a boy.

The doctors succeeded in working the clot down below the knee, but, after that, Papa's leg turned gangrenous and a decision was made to amputate. So Papa was taken to Freedmen's Hospital, which lay on both sides of Bryant Street, N.W, between 4th and 5th. On the south side was the administration building, which had recently been converted from a dental infirmary where we used to go to have our teeth examined. The sick were actually housed in two story cottages, which lined the north side. I can remember going to the administration building and having the receptionist ask who I wanted to see. We were then given a pass and told to which cottage we were to go. Papa's operation was successful. He was soon fitted with an artificial limb and soon he was walking and riding his bicycle. The only thing different about his walk was that one foot went down a little heavier than the other. One could detect this when one listened to his footsteps. Pop was eternally grateful to his doctors. I do not remember the name of the senior doctor, but his assistant was Dr. William Warfield, whom Papa hailed as a promising young man.[21]

People seldom went to the hospital in those days. Usually medical care was provided by members of the societies of which people were members. It was a sort of

---

[21] William Alonza Warfield, Sr. (1866-1951), served as Surgeon-in-Chief at Freedmen's Hospital from 1901 to 1936.

health insurance which guaranteed that in time of sickness one would be provided with around-the-clock nursing care. On another occasion, Papa fell ill with typhoid, and the society of which he was a member sent men who stayed with him all night. They were not professionals but ordinary citizens who had to go to work the next morning. But not only would they nurse him, they would bring food also. I remember that if one became ill with pneumonia, they would grease the patient, cover him (or her) with flannels and irrigate the nose and gargle the throat. Almost the same thing that is now provided simply by the taking of certain drugs was accomplished by these painstaking procedures. But it usually worked. But it did not in three instances when I was ten, which shook me severely.

In October, 1891 Aunt Kate, my father's younger sister, died at the age of 32. I do not know of what she died. Such things were not discussed in those days.[22] But I was struck with awe at seeing her body, covered with a sheet, lying on a slab in the parlor of her home with tubs of ice underneath. It was such an eerie sight and gave me an unnatural feeling that I cannot really describe as fear. I remember the undertaker coming three times a day to replace

---

[22] According to her death certificate, Kate Harvey, like many of Mrs. Tucker's relatives, died of tuberculosis.

the ice to keep the corpse from spoiling. It was not until the day of the funeral that it was placed in a coffin.

The very next month, little Lee Roy became ill with the croup. He was a fat, round-faced child, and it those days it was said that fat children had a very difficult time with the croup. I remember running to the drugstore to get medicine for him. Then I was in the bedroom upstairs where Mom sat, holding him in her arms, when suddenly he leaned forward, stretched out, and was still. "He's gone," Mom said very quietly. I ran downstairs, crying, "Lee Roy's dead!" I can never get his death out of my mind. I never want to see anything like that again. He was such a bright, such an active, such an intelligent little boy. For a long time I could not believe he was really dead. I thought he must somehow be alive underground. But he was dead.

I was very fond of my youngest sister, little Corinne. I remember that she had very fair skin. Nettie and I had named her. Our first choice was Louise, because we wanted to call her "Weezie," but Mom did not like that told us to choose again. So we settled on the name Corinne. But the happy days when I took Corinne in my arms and followed the organ grinder to all the saloons soon came to an end. A couple days after Christmas, when she was six months old, she died of pneumonia. I remember her baby casket being placed in the front seat of a hack and taken to the Old Harmony Cemetery [23] on Rhode Island Avenue, N.E.

---

[23] Now a Metro parking-lot.

Chapter III A Christian Household

Mom and Papa had by then lost four young children. However, they bore these losses with great resignation and tranquillity. I attribute this to one fact that they were both persons of deep religious faith. Ours was indeed a Christian home. Every Sunday after our regular family prayers we all went to the Second Baptist Church. I still have vivid recollections of that church and its members. The minister of the church in those days was William Bishop Johnson, usually called simply "Bishop" Johnson, as if his middle name were an ecclesiastical title. He was a tall, slender man, light in complexion, a native of Canada and highly educated. He was an excellent preacher, delivering straight-forward sermons, well-delivered in the best of English. I never knew what it was to listen to a preacher who had this peculiar way of catching his breath until I lived in the North. But, when Bishop Johnson advertised the subject of his sermon, as he often did, the church would be filled on Sunday, not only with members, but with visitors, white and colored, who often included senators and congressmen. Bishop Johnson was well-known and highly-regarded all over Washington.

Unfortunately, however, Bishop Johnson had a double personality. He could not withstand certain temptations. He had a horse and buggy which he used as he went on certain rounds. The horse knew well where to stop, so much so that when another pastor was with him in his carriage, the horse automatically stopped where Bishop Johnson did not want him to. Red-faced, he used the whip, shouting to the horse, "Why are you stopping here? Go on! Go on!" But the horse knew where to stop.

    I still remember the members of the congregation. We had an excellent choir and one of the soloists, who was called "Madame" Drew, was a beautiful woman with a most beautiful voice. There is another member of the church whose memory is fresh in my mind. I no longer remember her name. Some people have to do certain things to feel important. Now, in those days no woman felt dressed unless she wore silk skirts and undergarments so stiff that they rattled. Now this member was very, very dark and good-looking and always wore a stylish black dress of the highest fashion. She would come up a pair of steps to the door of the sanctuary. And the she got herself poised. I used to watch her as she placed one hand on her hip. Then, she would proudly come up the aisle with her husband beside her, her silken skirts just crackling! It was the highlight of her week. This was a relic of slavery. Some of the former slaves were so used to not having anything that when they acquired some substance they tended to overdo things. But it apparently did something for the ego of this person and the many others who were like her.

There is another member whom I remember well, and that was Attorney Robert D. Ruffin (1849-1905), one of the first graduates of Howard University. He was a nicely-built very black man. He conducted on Sunday afternoons what he called a "Lyceum." Apparently a man with extensive connections, he engaged nationally-known speakers for each event. I can vividly remember seeing a horse-drawn carriage stop at the church and Lawyer Ruffin step down in the company of a distinguished member of Congress. I do not remember any more the names of any of the white celebrities who addressed "The Forum", but I do remember some of the colored men who were or had been congressmen. There was Blanche K. Bruce[24], who had served as Senator from Mississippi. He was a very large, distinguished-looking man, very, very light in color. He was then serving as Register of the Treasury. He lived on Corcoran Street (which extended east between, between 14th and 16th Streets, N.W.), between Q and R, where many of Washington's "big wigs" lived at that time. Then there was John Mercer

---

[24] Blanche Kelso Bruce (1841-1898), U.S. Senator from Mississippi 1875-1881

Langston[25], who had served as a Congressman from Virginia. I remember him as a spare, light copper-skinned[26] man. Then there was John Roy Lynch[27], who had once been a member of the House from Mississippi. I also remember the Rev. Hiram Revells[28], a Methodist minister who became the first black man in American history to serve in the U.S. Senate. Robert Smalls[29] also spoke in our church. He had recently been a representative from South Carolina. He was the grandfather of my good friend, Mrs. Elizabeth Bamfield Hall. He was a big heavy man, very dark in color. I also remember Benjamin Sterling Turner[30], a representative from Alabama. I do not know whether he was related to my great-

---

[25] John Mercer Langston (1829-1897), an attorney and educator, who served as a U.S. Representative from Virginia from 1890 to 1891.

[26] Actually, Mrs. T. said, "About the color of your aunt [Louise Hubbard]."

[27] John Roy Lynch (1847-1939), Speaker of the Mississippi House of Representatives, the Republican served in Congress from 1873-1877 and 1882-1883.

[28] Hiram Rhodes Revells (1822?-1901) He served as U.S. Senator from Mississippi from 1870 to 1871, and later was president of Alcorn College in the 1870s and 1880s.

[29] Robert Smalls (1839-1915) served on the South Carolina legislature and was in the U.S. House of Representatives from 1875 to 1879, 1882-1883, and 1184-1887.

[30] Benjamin Sterling Turner (1825-1894), Republican Representative from Alabama 1871-1873.

grandmother or not (my oldest brother was named for him). He was a native of North Carolina, had been born a slave, but, by clandestine study, had obtained a good education and had become a prosperous businessman in Alabama before being elected to a term in Congress. They said he was quite wealthy. Then there was Calvin Chase[31], the owner and editor of the controversial colored paper, The *Washington Bee*. I remember Papa and his friend discussing that paper, quite radical for its time. "The *Bee* really does sting!" they would say. Chase, in fact, alienated many blacks with his militancy. When he died, his family wanted him buried from the Fifteenth Street Presbyterian Church, but its pastor, Dr. Francis James Grimke, whom I will tell more about later, refused to conduct his funeral services. Dr. Norman, pastor of Metropolitan Baptist Church, preached the sermon. And then I remember Henry Cheatham[32] I do not remember Frederick Douglass ever speaking at our Lyceum, but I went to his funeral in February, 1895, when I was in high school. It was held at the Methodist Episcopal Church between 15th and 16th Street, on M Street. I was unable to get into the

---

[31] William Calvin Chase (1854-1921), a Washington attorney who edited the *Washington Bee* from 1882 until his death. His motto was "Honey for friends, stings for enemies."

[32] Henry Cheatham (1857-1935), a Republican member of the U.S. House from 1889-1893, served as the Recorder of Deeds for the District of Columbia from 1897 to 1901.

church for the crowds of people of all colors there. When Anna Cooper[33], a noted educator, spoke at the Lyceum, a man got up and said something about being "an educated fool." She retorted, "I'd rather be an educated fool than an ignorant fool!"

Anderson Taylor, Pastor of Shiloh Baptist Church, which was then at 16th and L Streets, N.W. would speak at our Lyceum. Later something went wrong and he was removed from his charge. Then there was Walter Brooks, Pastor of the Nineteenth Street Baptist Church. He was very well-thought of. Other ministers were Rev. Stuart of Jezreel Baptist Church, Mr. Loving, Secretary of the local Baptist convention, and William "Red" Robinson, pastor of a church in Southwest. He was no scholar, but very influential. Robinson and several others of these pastors lived on DeFreese Street, N.W., near the Capitol, which was known as the "Street of Preachers."[34]

---

[33] Anna Julia Haywood Cooper (1858-1904) was principal of M Street High School in the early 1900s (after Mrs. T. was there).

[34] The street, which no longer exists, was in Swampoodle, near St. Aloysius Church, and ran from North Capitol west, for one block, to First Street, N.W.

One of the ministers I remember well was the Rev. George W. Lee,[35] pastor of the Vermont Avenue Baptist Church at Vermont Avenue, between R and Q Streets, N.W. He was absolutely black in complexion and monstrously fat. It is said that he would take a whole shoulder of meat in his hands and eat it right from the bone. Anyway, one day he went to call on one of his parishioners and fell off his bicycle[36] on the curb in front of his house, and was unable to rise until an army of passersby assisted him to his feet. A neighbor, observing the accident, immediately went into the member's house, inquiring whether she had ordered a ton of coal.

"A ton of coal? Why, no?"

"There's a ton of coal lying in front of your house."

The Rev. Lee was a very brilliant man and fine speaker. He would sleep soundly through meetings, yet somehow he knew everything that was said. It was said that he eventually ate himself to death and that his body was still purging in the coffin.

---

[35] George Wellington Lee (1852-1910), pastor of Vermont Avenue Baptist Church from 1885 to 1910. A contemporary said his skills as a preacher and orator were "commensurate with his vast bulk."

[36] On one occasion Mrs. Tucker said the Rev. Mr. Lee fell getting out of his carriage. Mary Gibson Hundley (1897-1986) also recalled Lee and said that owing to his size he was unable to use a normal, enclosed buggy and had one specially constructed to accommodate his generous girth.

My parents impressed on us that at some point we would have to make a conscious decision to "become Christians." I made my decision in the autumn of 1893, when I was 12 years old. Every fall, churches would have a month-long revival with nightly meetings. Those who wanted to "get religion" would go to what was known as the "Mourner's Bench" and pray, while the rest of the congregation sang and prayed. There would be preaching and exhortation. The members would sing over the candidates and pray over them. After a while, one of the candidates would stand up, and then another, proclaiming that they were "saved." Then the worshipers would become very happy. Relatives of the remaining "mourners" would stand over them and pray and talk softly to them. After a while, more "mourners" would stand up and profess a change. Many conversions were, to say the least, quite noisy. Sometimes some of the "saved" from some churches would continue shouting even after they left church and awakened the whole neighborhood with their cries of joy.

My conversion was relatively quiet. I went to the "Mourner's Bench" during the revival meeting, but nothing happened to me there. One night I went into our kitchen and prayed in the dark. All at once there was a feeling of elation that came over me. It was unnatural. I never had such a feeling before. I went into the room where my parents were and immediately they noticed the difference in me, but said nothing. I felt that for the first time I had communicated with God way down deep within me. The next night I went to church and made my profession publicly.

I immediately began to teach Sunday School and was assigned to the primary class. There was an older member of the church named Sister Dent who sat in the class to see that the children were quiet while I taught them. We had little cards with pictures on them with questions and answers, which made it very easy for a young teacher. That was the beginning of an active involvement with Christ's church that is still continuing more than eight decades later.

Chapter IV My Teenaged Years

Now Papa and Mom, being arch-Baptists, were against our attending the theater. Moreover, they were against dancing and we were absolutely forbidden to go to public dances, but we danced at home without their knowing it. When they went to their lodge meetings (we knew the dates), two or three girls or boys would come in and we would take up the rug and dance. Later on, Mom and Pop acquiesced to the point that they allowed Marietta, Ben, and me to earn money by playing at private dances. Many of the colored elite would have formal dances for a guest list of from 24 to 32 persons. Since the Harvey Family were well known as musicians throughout the greater part of Northwest Washington—we were dubbed "The Musical Harveys"—we were always in demand. For such occasions we were called upon to furnish the music. Usually the piano, violin, and cornet were adequate for such occasions. Marietta played the piano, Ben the violin, and a Mr. Holmes the cornet. Many times when there were two engagements on the same date, Pop would let me go, at which time Ben would engage a violinist and cornetist to play with me. This happened several times The one occasion that I remember most vividly was a gala affair which was staged by a group called the "Epicureans", which was comprised of some of the most outstanding colored citizens of Washington. It was held in what was then the fashionable suburb of Eckington (now very much the inner-city), where many of the colored aristocracy then had their palatial homes. Just a child, I was awed by the splendor and magnificence of the elegant house where we played for a company of 32 people. A sumptuous feast ensued.

How well do I remember the dances of those days! There was the schottisch —a very beautiful dance. Each couple would form a line and to the music sway to one side and to the other and then bow. When a dance floor of couples were in line, the women dressed in their beautiful silk and satin dresses of the day, the men in full dress, it was a beautiful sight to behold. Then there was the quadrille and the lancers, which were delightful square dances for four couples. The waltz was very popular also. The waltzes of Johann Strauss were very popular at the time. All of those dances were dignified in their performance. Oh, how I loved to play the orchestra score for piano!

We never lost our devotion or loyalty to the church, for whenever there was congregation in need of a full-time organist or a substitution, the Harveys were called upon. . When barely a teenager, Marietta was employed as organist of John Wesley A.M.E. Zion Church. While there, she married in her early 20s, to a lawyer named Marion

Clinkscales, and served there for many years thereafter. Later she became the organist of the Zion Metropolitan AME Church, located in Southwest Washington, remaining there until her retirement. Marietta also gave music lessons, and one of her pupils was Duke Ellington. She was his first music teacher. Later, she, when asked about him, she recalled, "He was just an ordinary, every-day student." In the early 1960s, Duke Ellington was in Washington and was interviewed on a radio station and spoke of his first teacher and expressed a desire to find out what had become of her. I at once contacted the radio station on which I heard the interview, to tell him that my sister had died.

When I was barely a teenager I often substituted for Marietta at John Wesley, and when I entered high school at 14 years old, I was the regular organist of the Metropolitan Baptist Church on R Street, between 12th and 13th Streets, N.W. When I was in high school I wrote and published a concert waltz and called it the "Rio Grande Waltz."

Ben was the organist of the Walker Memorial Baptist Church located on 13th Street, N.W., between U and V Streets When he was very young, he played in a band which often performed for funerals. In those days when a prominent person died—especially if he belonged to one or more of the societies and lodges, such as the Odd Fellows, Masons, Knights of Pythias, Good Samaritans and others, a band was hired to play. The band would form at their headquarters. A lot of these organizations had their headquarters in Southwest, and the band would march to the home of the deceased, accompany the funeral procession to the church, then to the cemetery and back to its headquarters. I remember the funeral of a boy who played the saxophone. Somebody marched in the procession, holding the saxophone on a black cloth. In these funerals, all along the way, from the beginning of the march, as soon as the band struck up, more and more people would stop anything they were doing and follow it. It was quite a sight. Here were some barefoot, some with one shoe on, some partly dressed, some with part of their hair combed and the comb in the other part of their hair, following the band all the way and back. When I grew older, I realized that these people, who had recently come from the backwoods of Maryland and Virginia, had a genuine love for music. There was no radio, no television, no phonograph in those days, and to follow a funeral band was really the only way many of these folk had a chance to hear band music. The music did something to their very souls—they were drawn as if by magic to follow the band. One impressive thing was that there was no rowdiness or yelling to each other, no dancing, rather, for the greater part of the time they were solemn. When the body was in the church, no sound was heard from those on the outside.

Many have asked me if I remember ragtime, which is now enjoying quite a revival nowadays. When I was in high school, syncopated music, especially the "Cakewalk", was first coming into vogue. I often played the piano in the assembly hall at school, and one day when I went to the music store to buy some new music, the clerk showed me a new pieces which was in Ragtime, but I would not take it, feeling that it was out of line for school purposes. However, not too much later, a student by the name of James Europe[37] played that very piece in assembly, with good effect. After that, I bought the piece. But Ragtime really became popular after I left Washington and was living in rural areas where that type of music never caught on.

I never thought of myself as an attractive girl. I always thought of my two sisters as better-looking than I. Marietta was small and petite and Nettie was medium height and considered "finely built", with the full figure that was admired during those years. Both of them had Mom's beautiful hair. I, however, was straight-up-and-down. At fourteen, I stood 5'7"[38]—taller even than my brothers—and weighed 145 pounds. Moreover, my hair was very fine and

---

[37] James Reese Europe (1881-1919) became a well-known band-leader and composer.

[38] She would eventually grow to 5'8½ and during most of her life, she weighed 185.

soft and would break off before attaining any length. Throughout my childhood, I was called "nappy-haired Rose Harvey" when some of the girls became mad at me. But, academically and musically, I always excelled my sisters. While they tended to look to Papa for advice about every detail of their lives, I was surprisingly independent. Papa recognized early that his "Rosebud", and would remark to his friends that, out of all his children, it was only I who never came to him, asking, "Pop, what shall I do?" but took my own initiative. As I said before, Marietta became a little jealous of me, but, Ben once remarked, "God knew what he was doing he didn't give Rose hair, for we wouldn't be able to do a thing with her if He had!"

After the eighth grade, I entered the old M Street High School, then the only colored high school in the Washington area and one of the finest secondary schools in all the Eastern United States. Boys and girls would come from miles away to go there. My sister Marietta had gone there and graduated when before the course was lengthened from three years to four. One of the students there was Garnet C. Wilkinson[39], who later became the superintendent of the colored schools. In later life, when I was into civic

---

[39] Garnet C. Wilkinson (1879-1969), a native of South Carolina, as First Assistant Superintendent of the D.C. Public Schools from 1924 to 1951, was in charge of the colored schools.

work, we had many pleasant conversations together. He would reminisce how he used to walk from his home in Anacostia every morning and back every evening. Inasmuch as the high school was located in the central city, and Anacostia was located in the far Southeast section, across the Anacostia River, Mr. Wilkinson had a walk of many miles. But he was not alone. The student population not only came from all sections of the city, but from Maryland as well, and from Alexandria, Arlington, and Hall's Hill in Virginia. The students from Virginia had to take the ferry boat from Alexandria to Washington and walk from the wharf to the M Street High School in all kinds of weather, a trek of many miles.

It was at M Street, that I was no longer known as Rose Harvey, but as "Miss Harvey." After one entered high school in those days, one was no longer addressed familiarly. People in those days generally did not address each other by their given names, unless they were relatives or close friends.

When I was in the lower grades, I just went to school. I did well, but I wouldn't say I was particularly interest, but when I got to high school I came into my own. There was nothing inspiring about the building, but there were boys and girls from all parts of the city and there was something that stirred in me and I said, "Now, here, I can do as well as the rest of them." I just picked up. English, Geometry, Algebra were required, and I took Latin, which was an elective, and I am glad that I did.

When I was a student at M Street, we were honored to have Paul Laurence Dunbar (1872-1906), the leading colored poet of the day, presented to us in our assembly hall. Then in his twenties, he was about the average height— about 5'8"-- very, very dark, slender, and very neat. He was very pleasant to meet, and, of course, we were all amazed by his recitations, some of which were in "dialect" and others in literary English. In 1916 when M Street High School moved to a new building, it was renamed for Paul Laurence Dunbar.

It was while I was in high school that my great-grandmother, Mildred Ruffin, died. She was almost 102 years old and was never in the least senile and was not sick until four months before her death in December, 1897.

Around the same time, we discovered our maternal grandmother. After Mom's father died, her mother remarried to Henry Thompson, a farmer of Louisa County, Virginia, and the family drifted apart. One sister went to live in Norfolk, Virginia, and another, Alice, made her home in Yonkers, New York. One day, Mom's oldest sister came to visit us. After she left, she wrote back, but her handwriting was so poor that none of us could understand the letter or even make out her address. Upon inquiry, we heard that she went to North Carolina to live, and we lost track of her forever. It was not long afterwards that my grandmother[40] took it upon herself to find out where her daughter Henrietta lived. Coming from Louisa County to Alexandria, she walked from the wharf into the District, asking everyone she met if they knew where "Levi" Harvey lived. By that time my parents owned a house at 121 K Street, N.W., and, by a miracle, she found us. When my sister Nettie opened the door, Grandmother immediately knew she was at the right home. "Get out the way!" she said. "I know you're Henrietta's daughter." Grandmother was a tall, strongly-built woman with our family's "Madagascar Hair." She was a very entertaining person. When living in the country, she was always sent for in time of sickness. She had her own name for various diseases: I remember once she diagnosed someone's illness as "dew poisoning." Eventually, she and her husband and Aunt Alice came to make their home in Alexandria, Virginia, and often Nettie and I took the ferry boat from Washington to visit them. Grandmother remained active and vigorous until three years before her death at 97 in 1923, when she entered the Stoddard Baptist Home.

---

[40] According to her death certificate, Caroline "Tompson" was a native of Montgomery County, Maryland.

Chapter V I Fall in Love

When I was a junior in high school, the Spanish-American War broke out. My brother Ben, then 20, went to war and became Chief Musician in the 48th Infantry Band, where he played the clarinet. That summer I went to Yonkers, New York, to visit Aunt Alice. Yonkers was considered "country" in those days by New Yorkers. I taught Sunday School in the "Colored Baptist Church" there. One Sunday they had a guest preacher by the name of Dr. James D. Corrothers. Another minister was supposed to fill the pulpit for the vacationing pastor that day, but, at the last minute he canceled and asked Dr. Corrothers to speak in his place. Dr. Corrothers got lost and was late arriving at the service, but he did speak, and delivered a very fine sermon. After that, we had afternoon Sunday School.

I was in the Senior Class, which Dr. Corrothers was teaching. The lesson was from the book of Exodus. Someone answered, but failed to explain the precise meaning of the word. "That is good, but what does the word *exodus* mean?"

Since Yonkers was "out in the country", New Yorkers thought of its inhabitants as ignorant bumpkins. I thought Dr. Corrothers must have been feeling the same way. I thought to myself, "Oh, yes, you think we are out here in the country and don't know anything." So, I spoke up and said, "'Exodus' means 'departure.'"[41] Dr. Corrothers was flabbergasted, especially when I was able to tell him precisely what Latin form it was. After that, several other questions came up that I was able to answer by understanding the Latin root. After class, Dr. Corrothers asked someone who I was, and was told "Miss Harvey from Washington."

That evening, he spoke again at the church. After I had left the church to go home, one of the church officers said to me, "Miss Harvey, did you speak to the minister and tell him that you enjoyed the sermon?"

I told him that I had not.

"Well," said he, "you were sitting right there in the choir, playing the organ. Don't you think he would appreciate your saying something to him?"

So I went back into the church and spoke to him. In the course of the conversation that followed, he told me that he was a writer and that he would like to send me one or two of his poems. I still thought he look down on me from the country, so I countered by saying that I had written some

---

[41] Actually, Mrs. Tucker said, "'Exodus is a Latin word and it comes from 'ex' means 'out' and 'eo', which means 'go.'" "*Eo*" is not the Latin word for "go", and "Exodus" is actually a Greek word, so I am making the assumption that actual conversation was as I have reconstructed it.

music and would like to have him hear it. So, that is how we became acquainted, and very soon, after that, do you know what happened? We were married! I was not quite seventeen at the time.[42]

Looking back over my life, I am struck at how all things have worked according to God's will. Had it not been for my decision to taken Latin, I probably would never have become acquainted with the man who became my husband. Then, too, even though I had only one more year to complete my high school course when I married, I have concluded that this too, was the best for me. Not that I do not believe in a person obtaining as much education as one can (my son had three degrees and was working on his Ph.D. when he died), but if, for some reason, it does not work out that one can obtain a complete formal education, God can still use us. As it turned out, it was to my benefit that I never finished M

---

[42] Mrs. Tucker evidently was unwilling to disclose all the circumstances of her marriage. During the interviews, she stated that she was married in Niles, Michigan, but omitted the statement in her latest version of the autobiography. According to the U.S. Census of 1900, on June 5 of that year, she was living as a single woman with her parents on K Street in Washington. James D. Corrothers was enumerated June 8 in Red Bank, New Jersey. He was described as a widower, and was living with a five year old son, Willard. Henry, who was born in December, 1899, is nowhere to be found in the 1900 Census. The 1910 census found James and Rosina Corrothers living in Washington, DC. According to that census, they had been married 11 years and Henry was 10 years old. In the 1910 census, Henry's birthplace was given as "Virginia." His death certificate, for which his mother was the informant, states that he was born in Washington, DC.

Street High School. Had I done so, no doubt I would have become a school teacher. I would have gone to Normal School and then began a teaching career, like so many of my classmates. In a way, this would have been quite an accomplishment. To the people just a generation removed from slavery, to be a school teacher was quite an accomplishment. During bondage many slaves had an insatiable desire to learn how to read and write, and this passion to learn increased immeasurably after freedom. The Christian minister and the school teacher were highly respected persons and their dedication to teaching the newly-freed people has its place in Negro history. During that period students truly learned reading, writing, and arithmetic. Also, parents disciplined their children at home, so, when they entered school, the teacher did not have to use valuable time for disciplinary tasks but could completely concentrate on teaching.

In later years, new courses were added to the school's curriculum—most non-essential—and new methods were established and teachers were taught what to teach, how to teach it, and even what to think, to the effect that they were fashioned as if in the same mold. Some teachers today are unable to think for themselves and in discussions they have nothing constructive to submit; in fact, they are reticent to express an opinion because of their inability to formulate one of their own.

By marrying young and by marrying Dr. Corrothers, I got a practical education, which was much broader and fuller than that which I would have gotten by graduating from high school and entering teachers' college and then pursuing a teaching career. My traveling and my contacts were such that my horizons were broadened and I observed events and conditions from different angles. I learned to study a subject, analyze it, and come to my own conclusion. I developed the art of thinking for myself. I came in contact with people who had an aptness to analyze and discuss momentous events of our times and who were ever striving for self-improvement. Such contracts were incentives to me and an education that has enabled me to cope with those who have diplomas from high schools, normal schools, colleges, and universities. All this is simply to say that if we commit our way to the Lord, everything works out for the best. God can use whatever we bring to Him to cause us to serve some useful purpose. And that has been the case with me.

Chapter VI—James David Corrothers

Dr. Corrothers and I were not just husband and wife—we were close friends and companions. He never wanted to do anything without first getting my opinion, and he never wanted to go any place without me. We had mutual interest and understanding. I called him "Poet" and his name for me was "Rosa Greena", for one day someone asked our younger son Henry what his mother's name was. Not knowing how t say "Rosina", he responded in his father's hearing, "My mother's name is Rosa Greena." Ever after that, Poet called me "Rosa Greena", which he later shortened to "Greena."

Poet was about 5'8½" tall and weighed 185 pounds. A muscular man, he had been quite a runner and boxer when younger. While I was married to him, he made it a practice of walking fast and juggling Indian clubs and lifting weights. He detested football, though, and never wanted our sons to play that sport. He was a handsome man. He inherited his light brown complexion from his Cherokee ancestors. It is a funny thing about a Cherokee—he changes his complexion according to his mood. I noticed that sometimes there would be a brownish tint to his color, at other times I detected a reddish glow. His hair fell in long loose ringlets down the sides of his face and head.

Poet was one of the greatest preachers I have heard, and I record this not just because he was my husband. He had studied elocution at Northwestern and developed a highly trained delivery. He used a variety of effective gestures. He could stand in the pulpit and turn to the side and paint on the wall the most beautiful word picture one could imagine. Although some of his opponents called him an "actor," many people loved his sermons. When he died, an Episcopal priest asked me for copies of his sermons. But I had to tell him that I had only outlines, as Poet had never written out his sermons. Thus, his messages have been lost to posterity.

Poet's story is an interesting one. He was born July 2, 1869, in the "Chain Lake Settlement" of former slaves in Cass County, Michigan. His mother, who was born in Ohio, died when he was born. His father remarried and gave "Jimmy" to his grandfather to rear.[43]

---

[43] According to U.S. Census of 1880, James D. Corrothers, age 9, was living in Van Buren County, Michigan, with his father, James R. Corrothers, (age 35, a native of Ohio),a farmer, his mother (or stepmother) Harriet, 27,and his siblings Sarah (12), Edward W. (8), Norman W. (6), Oscar R. (3), and Minnie (born May, 1880) According to the census of 1900, James and Harriet had four more children, including Alford (b. 1883), Frances (b. 1890), and Effie (born 1891). Sarah and James seem to have been the children of the first of James R's three wives.

. "Grandfather", although of Scots and Cherokee ancestry, was nevertheless considered "colored." Besides him and other relatives, Poet had little contact with members of his race during his boyhood, which was spent in the tiny lumbering town of South Haven. Poet was regarded as an object of curiosity by some white people. Once, while passing a farm house, the farmer ran out and stopped him and asked him to "wait in the road a minute" until he could get his little son, who had "never seen a *colored* boy before." When he child appeared, he asked Poet why his face was dirty. When he replied, "I'm not dirty, I'm *colored*. God made me this way," the child asked, "But how can you tell when your face is dirty?"

Poet grew up in great poverty and lived through the terrible race riots against the few Negroes in South Haven. To the day of his death, he remembered the terrible cries: "Fifty cents for a nigger! A dollar for a nigger! Just one more nigger!" Negroes had to hide in the woods, the graveyards, and under the raised wooden sidewalks, but he survived and went to work in the mills of Muskegon, Michigan, at 14. He was a "carnivorous" reader, and eager "devoured" every book he could lay his hands upon. He began to compose verse. One day, while working as a boot-black in Chicago, he happened to shine the shoes of a man whom he recognized as a distinguished person and with whom he began to discuss literature. During the conversation, Poet told him that he wrote poetry, and when he produced some samples, the stranger asked to take them with him. The stranger turned out to be Henry D. Lloyd, part owner of the *Chicago Tribune*, who published one of his poems, called "The Soldier's Excuse." Mr. Lloyd obtained a position for him in the paper's counting room and the salary was the most pay he ever had until that time.

While employed by the *Tribune*, Poet contributed many articles and poems to various metropolitan magazines and journals. He collected folk tales from Negroes who had migrated from the deep South to Chicago. This collection was published by Funk and Wagnall's. He also interviewed the "leading Negroes" of Chicago and wrote an article on them.

Poet was attending Northwestern University when he was persuaded by Charles W. Grandison, President of Bennett College, in Greensboro, North Carolina, to enroll as a student in that institution. He taught Dr. Grandison's classes when he was away. It was here that Poet established a Department of Physical Culture, one of the first in a Negro college. He sent to Chicago for a weight-machine, punching bag, and Indian clubs and dumb bells. While he was in North Carolina, he gave many weight lifting exhibitions.

Poet was not satisfied by the quality of education he was getting at Bennett College. There was one professor in particular, whose "Negro mannerisms and lapses of dignity impressed me unfavorably," he later wrote. "I had always abominated these things and did not relish sitting under a man of this type." So, with the financial assistance of a benefactor, Miss Frances Willard[44], he returned to Evanston, re-enrolled at Northwestern, and eventually graduated.

After graduation, Poet was working as a journalist when he came to know James Whitcomb Riley, the "Hoosier Poet" and Paul Laurence Dunbar, "The Poet of the Race." He married Fannie Clemens of Chicago, a minister's daughter. She bore him a son, whom they named Willard Dumas Corrothers, after his benefactress and the black French writer.[45] Shortly after the birth of a second son, Richard, the first Mrs. Corrothers died, followed by the infant a few months later.

Shortly before that time, Poet had experienced a great change in his life. He had for some years been completely "turned off" by the church. One day he was passing a church in Chicago and, as usual, felt an "inexpressible disgust", as

---

[44] Frances Willard (1839-1898) Educator, suffragist, and head of the Women's Christian Temperance Union.

[45] Alexandre Dumas (1802-1870)

he felt that the church "enthralled my race to ancient things instead of encouraging it to absorb the progressive and beneficial ideals of the present era.." Suddenly, however, he had a change of heart. He described it this way: "A sunburst fell upon my being. My soul seemed revived. I was aglow with a new delight. My soul was satisfied." Immediately after this experience, he decided to enter the ministry of Christ, convinced that "the cause of righteousness needed honest men." Having joined the Baptist denomination in New York City, he became a "local preacher."

His pastor helped him to secure engagements as a supply minister and it was while functioning thus that I met him. Together with his writing and speaking engagements, he was doing very well financially. Within a year of our marriage, we moved to Washington, DC, where I gave birth in December, 1899, to my only child, whom we named Henry Harvey Corrothers, named in honor of my mother (Henrietta Harvey). To my great regret, I was never able to have any more children. In later years he was known as Hank Corrothers, the athlete.

Willard, the surviving son of Dr. Corrothers' first marriage, who had been living in New Jersey, came to live with us as soon as we were settled. I never spoke of Willard as a stepson, but as my own. My husband was ordained a Baptist minister in the Second Baptist Church of

Washington, the church where I had been baptized and to which all my family belonged.

Chapter VII—South Haven, Michigan

For a while we lived in Washington, and we were there when President McKinley was assassinated. I don't remember anything about it, except that it happened. I do not think it made any impact on me. I wasn't too interested in politics at the time. I do remember reading that people, in droves, went to the rotunda of the Capitol to view his body.

What I do remember is that a few months later, I was substituting as organist at the Liberty Baptist Church on Connecticut Avenue, N.W., and I had to pass the White House. I was just going along when I saw these people stopping to look at this man who looked very distinguished and important. It was the President, Theodore Roosevelt. To my surprise the guards surrounded me and I didn't know what to think, so finally it came to me that I had a handkerchief in my hand[46], and that is why they surrounded me.

A few years went by and Poet received a letter from relatives in South Haven, Michigan, where he was reared and went to school (the only colored boy in town), that an uncle had died and left him some money and a herd of sheep. He

---

[46] President McKinley had been shot by a man with a pistol concealed under a handkerchief.

was advised to go to South Haven to protect his interest. He decided not only to go himself, but to take us with him. We truly enjoyed the long trip from Washington to Michigan. We were on our way to that part of Michigan known as the peach belt, for farmers owned acres and acres of peach trees. While riding on the train, hour after hour, we saw miles of peach trees, apple trees, and pear trees, and vineyards, all of which were so planted that, no matter from which angle one looked, they were in uniform rows. These farmers also cultivated what they called "small fruits", such as black and red raspberries, strawberries, currants, and others—all of which, I learned later, were government inspected. At the least sign of infection, the trees were ordered cut down and destroyed by fire, thus protecting the health of people.

We thought it best to make our first stop at Coloma, Michigan, where Poet's father, stepmother, and sister Effie lived. Coloma is only a few miles from South Haven. As the train neared the station, Poet asked me if I could see anyone who might be there to meet us. (I was sitting on the window side). I said, "Yes! I see a man who looks very much like you." It was his father. The father-son greeting was very emotional, as they had not seen each other since Jimmy was a very young boy. The boys and I loved Father and Mother Corrothers at sight, also Effie, the youngest child, Poet's half sister.

We moved to South Haven and, in time, he received a part of the money his uncle left him, but he was not able to find out what became of the sheep. While waiting for the completion of the investigation, Poet, at the insistence of some of the people, organized a much-needed church. We received some financial assistance from the townspeople and there were those who actually helped with the construction of the building whenever they could.

South Haven was the little town where Poet was reared, and some of the inhabitants had read his stories and poems in magazines. Therefore, when he returned to South Haven, he received a hearty welcome from his old schoolmates, who were now important members of the community, conducting its civic, municipal, judicial, and financial affairs. We were invited to every function of importance held in the city and surrounding communities and seated always at the guest table. There was no segregation in the city or the school and we freely communicated with and freely visited our neighbors, who were white.

I liked South Haven, for it was a beautiful little city, one part of which was a peninsula, surrounded on two sides by Lake Michigan and on the third by the Black River. I was surprised that the intensity of the roar of the waves of the lake was almost as great as that of the Atlantic Ocean. Soon, however, I became accustomed to it. The houses were cottages with many feet of space between them and with deep front and back yards, abundant with trees and shrubbery, some of which were beautiful all year round. When the fish were biting, it was noised around and it appeared that everybody quit what they were doing and went fishing for the day. The first summer we were in South Haven, there was a devastating hail storm when everyone was forced to fasten blankets over their windows to keep out the glass broken by the hail stones. We had also to spend the duration of the storm on our staircases for protection. The next morning there were hundreds of dead birds everywhere one looked. Everywhere the storm struck the gardens of corn, peas, tomatoes—in fact, all vegetation, small and large, was powdered into nothingness. Farmers suffered monetary losses as well as food for their families and their stock. It was a freak storm, striking only a part of the community.

The beach was about a ten minute walk from our home, and in the summer when we had time, we would walk along the beach or sit in the sand and watch the waves break towards the shore. Many of the town's people came to the beach. Several times we noticed a Japanese man standing on the beach. He was always alone. Finally, we had an opportunity to talk with him. He never disclosed why he was in that particular part of the country. He did not say that he was a student or that he was working in Chicago. During our conversation we asked him if he had discovered anything here in America that would be of service to the people of his country. He said, "Yes, many things. Whatever we find in any country we *Japanize* it." Our interpretation of this statement was that they added to what they had learned and deleted that which was not useful to them, and when their reconstruction was completed, they called it their own product—they had "*Japanized* it."

When we arrived in South Haven, a tourist business was being established, catering chiefly to vacationists from Chicago, which was a few miles away, directly across Lake Michigan. There were picnic areas, a roller coaster, a carousel, and a variety of other amusements. There was a beautiful excursion boat, the *Eastland*, which sailed from Chicago at night. Some vacationers remained a week or two or more.

All of the residents of the city were delighted when they heard afar across the lake the faint sounds of music from the calliope, which was on the very top deck of the boat, grow louder and louder as it neared the shore, and many people would be on the shore when the boat landed, to meet friends and relatives and to welcome tourists.

One day my husband and I went to the top deck of the *Eastland* and talked to the calliopist and he invited me to play it. I played it, but surprised the others around as well as myself, because it took very strong fingers to press against the number of pounds of steam necessary to bring out the tones. It was quite an experience for me. It was an accomplishment also for me as a woman.[47]

Poet and I gave entertainments in the white churches and school houses for the benefit of the church building, and people would stop now and then for a pleasant conversation. One such person had been to our home earlier to get an opinion on a literary matter. As they talked, Poet discovered that he was an agnostic. Nevertheless, the man promised to come to the church when it was completed. Not long afterwards, he arranged for us to give an entertainment at the school house in his community. On the day designated for the affair he drove to our home in his sleigh and took the four of us to his home in the country for dinner with his family. We then drove to the school house where we gave our concert. Poet contributed poems and stories from his own books and I gave the piano numbers. After spending the night with his family, we were brought home in the sleigh, laden with many kinds of vegetables and fruits.

I had the opportunity to do some teaching on the piano. My students were mostly white children, because they were the ones who had pianos. Worthy of mentioning

---

[47] In the summer of 1915, the *Eastland* rolled over, bottom side up, in the Chicago River, killing more than 800 passengers.

are two little girls, about 10 and 12 years old, neither of whose parents could speak or hear, although the girls could. It was an interesting and happy family. Their home was so built that they could see through to every room. I asked the mother how she reared her babies. She wrote simply, "God helped me." One day, after lessons were over, she asked me to play something for her. I thought, "I'll play a simple tune," but as I neared the piano I was inspired to do one of my best concert numbers. I was amazed at her enthusiasm, for at intervals she clapped her hands. I asked her if she could hear my playing. She said, "Yes." The vibrations from the piano went to the floor and came up from her feet through her entire body and that was how she heard the musical sounds.

There was a woman from an outlying community who would come to my home several times before Easter Sunday, Children's Day, and Christmas for me to coach her in playing the special music for those occasions for her Sunday School. I don't know how she found me, but, as these seasons came, there she was at my door, with her horse and buggy parked at my curb.

Not only did I enjoy the beach at South Haven in the summertime, but I enjoyed walking with my family out in the country in the fall, observing the farmers preparing their harvest of fruits and vegetables for various markets, the principle one being Chicago. I found many interesting things as we stopped here and there as we walked along. The one thing that I remember most vividly is the manner in which bushels and bushels of apples were pressed and how the clear fresh juice flowed into huge vats and was then bottled for the market.

In one of our walks we met a wealthy man who made his home in Chicago and, as a side-line, he had a farm on the outskirts of South Haven, where he raised many breeds of chickens, all fenced in, according to breed. It was interesting to know the history of each of the five breeds and how he came by them.

While I enjoyed my sojourn in Michigan, I had an aversion to the severe winters. Often it would begin to snow in September, and, if not then, surely in October, when it would often snow every day. The snow would drift and pack, drift and pack until February, when there was what was known as the "February Thaw", at which time one would at least see the ground, and sometimes all the snow would disappear. It would begin again and snow until April. The weather was very cold and it seemed as if it was always below zero. I wearied of these long, cold winters, so, when the little church was completed, I was eager to leave South Haven.

I learned much from living in South Haven and other towns and cities in the area, such as Dowagiac, Ipsilanti, Kalamazoo, and Jackson (the prison city). I added to my knowledge the differences in the habits, customs, and even the speech of the people, but the most important and lasting experience of my years in Michigan was meeting my husband's relatives, especially my father and mother-in-law and my sister-in-law, Effie Jane, who is now Mrs. Jane Corrothers Artis. I met a brother, Norman Corrothers, who at the time lived in Coloma. We visited another brother, Oscar, his wife and family, at St. Joseph, Michigan, a beautiful little city on the Lake. We visited a sister, Minnie Corrothers Boone in Benton Harbor as well as my husband's uncle, Daniel, his wife and son George at Battle Creek, the "Cereal City." We became friends, and after Poet died, I kept in touch with them until one by one, they died. Oscar's sons and daughters often write me and at times will call me, saying, "I want to hear your voice again." On February 4, 1977, Jane wrote me, saying that she had lost her husband and her two daughters and had moved to California to live with her son.

Chapter VII—We Move to Virginia

Around 1906 Poet obtained a pastorate in Lexington, Virginia, in the Shenandoah Valley. In recommending him, Dr. William Bishop Johnson wrote: "I want to say to the officers of the church that Rev. Corrothers is a rare combination: a man of many excellent parts...You will have a great Bible student and teacher, and a preacher whom you will like to hear more, if you call him to your pulpit."

There was a great deal of remembrance of "The War" there, for many of the old citizens had been slaves, which was evident from their subservience to white people. It was different with those who had been born after slavery or had never been slaves, for, having worked for members of the faculty, they had absorbed much of the culture of Virginia Military Institute (VMI) and the Washington and Lee University. I have observed this cultural impact in other university cities where I have lived.

During these years, Poet and I were frequently engaged by churches and other institutes to give concerts. I would give the piano numbers and Poet would recite a number of his poems and tell some of his stories. Some of his poems and stories were in literary English, and others were humorous, and in Negro dialect. My part of the program was varied, consisting of some Beethoven, Brahms,

Chopin, Friml, and Rachmaninoff. On some of our programs I would play Louis Moreau Gottschalk's "The Last Hope", a beautiful and difficult composition with many variations and embellishments. There is a setting of the hymn "Holy Spirit, Truth Divine", based on the them of "The Last Hope." Two appealing numbers of my program were descriptive:"The Storm" and "Listen to the Mockingbird." I also played the piano transcription of the sextette from Gaetano Donizetti's *Lucia di Lammermoor.* Later, I added compositions from contemporary composers Nathaniel Dett and Edward McDowell. At that time I could entertain for over three hours from memory.

I have always loved the waltz and at any time I could sit at the piano and improvise one. I wrote a concert waltz and played it for a soldier friend of my family, George M. Jones, who was a musician in the Tenth U.S. Infantry Band, which had been stationed at one time on the banks of the beautiful Rio Grande. So he suggested that I name this waltz "The Rio Grande Waltz." I published it and many copies were sold. Another musician, James Miner, a violinist, orchestrated it for his band and played it on many occasions for concert work and for dancing. I have also written a march and several hymns.

Soon after Poet arrived in Lexington, I was asked to give a concert alone. There was no piano in the church, so a member allowed the officials to move her own into the building for the concert. The committee planned this to be a big affair and sold tickets to white people as well as colored, and the church was crowded with both. In most churches there were pews in the front that ran parallel on both sides to the length of the church. These were called the "Amen Corner." When I entered the church for my performance, I noticed that many chairs had been added to the pews on the left aisle of the church and that this entire section was occupied solely by white people. I was told later that such seating *just had to be* in that manner. The concert was a success. Many were surprised at my performance. Everybody enjoyed it and the church was visibly proud of me.

In 1908 we returned to Washington and shortly thereafter, Poet was called to the pastorate of a large congregation in Westmoreland County, Virginia, known as "The Little Zion Baptist Church." We continued to live in Washington and travel by boat to Westmoreland County on the two Sundays when the church had services. We therefore had two full weeks to ourselves in Washington. During this time, Poet preached in the pulpits of many of the leading churches and taught Theology and Sacred Oratory in the Wilbanks Institute.

In 1906 167 U.S. colored soldiers had been discharged "without honor" for alleged rioting in Brownsville, Texas. Senator Joseph Foraker of Ohio continued to keep the issue alive through speeches and writings, and we were in the Senate gallery when, in April, 1908, the Senator made an eloquent plea on behalf of the discharged men, in which he contended, "They ask no favors because they are Negroes, but justice because they are men!" Poet wrote a poem in honor of Senator Foraker (who failed in his attempt at re-election that year) and sent him a copy:

> On that hot, barbed hill in Cuba,
> Where the Spaniards blocked the way,
> At San Juan, when brave men faltered,
> Our black soldiers saved the day.
> They were men like Mingo Sanders,
> Heroes of the camp and fight,
> Were they cowards down in Brownsville?
> Dread marauders in the night?
> Veterans bathed in holy battle,
> Where the dark Lethe rolled in sight!
> White Senator, put off the cares of State,
> Rest, Friend of Truth, known of the gods above.
> The storms broke over thee, but found thee great,
> Though time, white Time, has touched thee with his snow.
> To thy grand rest, like Cincinnatus go,
> With honors and with grateful love.

Soon Poet was offered a full-time pastorate in Westmoreland County. The people wanted us very badly. They offered Poet a pretty good salary and offered me a position as a school teacher. Moreover, they promised to build us a home as well as give us chickens and hogs and other livestock. But we had to consider our boys' education. Willard was then 14 and Henry was nine. They could not get a good education in rural Virginia and we did not want to send them away to school; we wanted them close at their young age. So we refused that offer and accepted a call to a church in Haverhill, Massachusetts. While we were in Haverhill, Poet published a story in the *American Magazine*, entitled "At the End of the Controversy," which was partially true. He received $100.00 for it. He also published several poems in the *Century Magazine*.

We were disappointed with New England. As was in the case in Michigan, the people were just not interested in religion. We had associated that part of the country with great *literati* such as Whittier, Emerson, and Longfellow, with "poets as far-visioned reformers", as Poet put it, but, instead we found, in Poet's words, "a large and assertive foreign population which had not caught New England's fine spirit nor imbibed any other than coarser Americanisms which one picks up in the streets. They have not...heard of Whittier or Emerson, but they were able gratuitously to inform me, with profane emphasis, that I was a nigger!" Even the New England Negroes were disappointing. Poet later wrote that he was "glad to resign and to get away from among them, where pastoring among colored Baptists, at least, is one long nightmare of fuss-dodging."

The second week of January, 1909, early in our stay at Haverhill, we returned to Washington for a visit and stayed at the home of friends. The evening we returned, we dropped in at my parent's home on K Street for a visit. Mom was there, but Papa was away from the house. I told Mom that we would see Papa in the morning. But the next morning Papa, who suffered from angina, which necessitated the administration of special medication, had a heart attack in his shop and died instantly. There was a laundry in the same building adjoining his shop, and Papa's Chinese friend who owned the laundry found him. He was only 57.

His obituary read:

Lee Roy Harvey departed this life on Saturday morning, January 9, 1909, at about 9:00. Though his death was very sudden and unexpected, we fully believe that he was thoroughly prepared for the great change; for he had been setting his "house in order" and laboring faithfully in his Master's cause for over forty years. He professed faith in the Lord Jesus Christ. He joined Second Baptist Church in 1870 and became a Deacon of the Church and helped to found Mount Olive Baptist Church when eight members of Second Baptist obtained letters to organized a needed church in Northeast. He returned to Second Baptist.

Chapter VIII—Our Boys

Poet and I were parents whose concern for our sons was that they lead a normal and useful life. We took care to provide them an environment conducive to clean living, polite speech, and proper attitudes towards everyone. We were a very close family. We perhaps did not have family devotions as much as one might expect. We had Bible readings and prayer on Sundays, but many families at that time had them every day. But evenings we would get together as a family to discuss things together. We often read to each other. When Willard and Henry were young, we read aloud to the from *The Swiss Family Robinson*, *Black Beauty*, and other books. When they got a little older, we would discuss the books and other serious topics.

I was very much concerned about my role as stepmother to Willard. I never used the term. I always tried to be careful that I showed no difference in work or action in my dealings with the boys. When Willard and Henry were little, I used to say jokingly that I used a tape measure to be sure that the portions served were equal. If there was the slightest difference, I made sure that it benefitted Willard. Thankfully, Henry never resented this.

In those days, the minister and his family were under strict scrutiny at all times. Many parishioners took delight in "picking" our children as to what went on in our home and in the church. We trained our sons to be aware of such maneuvers and to answer all questions in the nicest way possible, without giving information. Henry, though the younger, was adroit in such instances, but Willard, who was less patient, would have to watch himself closely to avoid telling them to mind their own business.

By the time Willard was ten and Henry was five years old, they had traveled more than most grownups. At that age, they had been to Chicago and many cities and towns in Michigan, to New York, New Jersey, Pennsylvania, Maryland, and Virginia. Traveling in itself was an education to them.

Our boys started in mixed schools in the North, and therefore, had no trace of Negro "dialect." Both boys were vocal concerning their travels, and wherever we lived, the people liked to converse with them. I would sometimes send them to the store, and when they were late returning home, they would tell me that someone had stopped to talk with them. When they were in the Washington schools here, during our first sojourn in my native city, the other students laughed at their northern accent when they recited their lessons. The teacher defended them, however, saying, "These boys speak English. You don't."

As teenagers, the boys gave us relatively little trouble. Willard would often sass me, but he was fiercely protective of me to the sometimes prying parishioners. I felt that God directed me in my rearing of them, and often He sent me intuitions which always proved right. For instance, Willard asked us for a bicycle. I discussed this with Poet, who asked me, "Why not?" I replied that I could not state a reason, "But I do not have a good feeling about it." But since we could not put our finger on any *logical* reason why he shouldn't have a bike, Poet gave him one. My intuition proved right, however, when this gift became an incitement to Willard to cut classes and ride off to the surrounding towns and villages. But, by and large, Poet and I had little trouble. This was probably because we saw to it that ours was a strong Christian home. We did things together as a family, and so the boys did not feel the need to seek amusement , to any large extent, away from home, with the possibility of getting into trouble.

Both our boys grew to be 6'2" tall. Willard was extremely fair of complexion with curly blond hair. Henry was light brown-skinned with hair like black velvet. At that time we remarked how the younger generation of that time tended to be noticeably taller than their parents. Both Willard and Henry were active and athletic, although their father forbade them to play football.

Chapter IX—Bereavement

After our experience at Haverhill, Poet and I were thoroughly disenchanted with the Baptist denomination. We went to Philadelphia, where a friend of Poet's, Dr. John W. Lee, pastor of the Germantown Presbyterian Church, talked to us and told us that the Presbyterian Church needed intelligent ministers and that Poet would, if he decided to join that denomination, receive credit for everything he had down. Although I had been born and reared a Baptist, I felt I could accept Presbyterianism. I asked Dr. Lee to explain the church doctrine and polity, and the only point on which I disagreed was concerning Baptism: I believe in Baptism by immersion. Since, however, I had already been immersed, it was no problem, as far as I was concerned.

Poet went right to work in West Philadelphia. I, as usual, gave music lessons. Poet wrote for periodicals in addition to his preaching. We got along very well. Around 1913, Poet received a call to the Second Presbyterian Church in West Chester, Pennsylvania, and accepted it. Here Poet worked very hard. He increased the membership, put in new furniture and carpets and installed central heating. At the same time, he preached his sermons and performed his pastoral duties and completed his second major book, an autobiography, *In Spite of the Handicap*. He trusted no one but Henry to mail the finished manuscript to the publisher, the George H. Doran Company in New York. He continued to write poetry and organized other of his works together, but died before he was able to publish them.

During our pastorate in West Chester, I formed a chorus of the best singers from all the churches and we sang such compositions as Handel's Halleluiah Chorus and the *Inflammatus* from Rossini's *Stabat Mater*. We also sang a choral arrangement of Johann Strauss, Jr.'s "Beautiful Blue Danube."

We were often invited to be present at outstanding events. On one occasion Dr. Corrothers was a platform guest of Dr. Billy Sunday[48] during his campaign in Philadelphia. The meetings were held in a huge tent. The ground was strewn with sawdust. When the invitation was given for those who wanted to be saved, they were asked to walk down the "sawdust trail" to the front of the tent. Dr. Sunday had many antics while he was preaching, one of which was suddenly to jump from the floor to the top of the pulpit. Crowds were at the tent services every day and night. Large baskets with handles were used for the collection of money and the baskets were always filled to the brim.

---

[48] William Ashley Sunday (1862-1935), a Presbyterian minister, was celebrated for his revival meetings.

During this time, Poet wrote articles about two outstanding schools. One was about the Cheyney Training School for Teachers, said to be the oldest such school in America. It was situated in a beautiful spot about 22 miles from Philadelphia. The other school was the Downingtown Industrial and Agricultural School, which had been established by generous colored citizens, to give boys and girls practical training in many vocations. It was then considered "another Tuskegee." These two articles appeared in the *Philadelphia Record* and were published in 1915 under the caption, "The School and Home." After many years of struggle, things seemed to be looking up.

Neither Poet nor I realized how heavily his schedule was bearing on his strength. One Monday I had worked extremely hard at my household chores and that night a choir rehearsal had been called to meet at our home. Some of the members could read music and others could not, but all were apt and all had good voices and loved to sing. The rehearsal lasted almost two hours. When it ended I was exhausted and went to bed and fell asleep immediately. My sleep was troubled, however, and I awoke in the middle of the night, as if in a daze, sensing that something was wrong. I turned and, to my horror, found Poet speechless and helpless by my side. Oh, the pain that pierced my heart! "Boys! Boys!" I called. "Your father is ill."

The neighbors came and the doctor came. Poet had suffered a major stroke that paralyzed his right side. The doctor worked on him, ordered medicine, and showed us how to wrap him in a blanket soaked with hot water. We did that for about a week and the church members perceived that I was on the verge of breaking down. "You can't last long," they said, "caring for Dr. Corrothers day and night." So, at their suggestion, I consented to his hospitalization. After a week or so, however, Poet wanted to come home, so I had him brought home and immediately he showed some improvement. He no longer had to have the hot blanket treatment. Willard and I had to massage him twice a day and I would help him stand and teach him to walk again, step by step. In a few months he could walk, supported by a cane. He had to learn to write left-handed. While his speech gradually returned, it was somewhat affected, but he was able to make himself understood.

While Poet was recovering from his stroke, there were many tense moments for me, because at times he would become discouraged about his slow recovery and would ask me if I thought he was improving. I would say, "Yes," and then he would ask, "Why do you think so?" Deep within me I would pray, "God, please help me to answer him in an encouraging manner," and then I would say, "Your speech is better." Another time, when asked, I would say, "You are walking better" or "You are using your right hand better" or "You can now type." When he asked me such questions, he would look at me, intently reading my every expression. Many times, after such questioning, I would go upstairs, fall upon the bed and weep and pray, for I myself was discouraged, too, but dare not let him know it, because, if I had showed weakness in any manner, he would have detected it and that would have been disastrous, because, to a large extent he depend on me for strength and looked to my faith to sustain him. Even before his illness, he would at times become very discouraged and comment, "I wish I had your faith!"

Eventually, Poet was able to resume a limited schedule and once again take the pulpit. On Sunday, February 4, 1917, however, while he was preaching, I became conscious of a change in his countenance. He preached an uplifting sermon, but, in the midst of it, he suddenly changed the trend of his thoughts and turned to the choir (to the left of the pulpit, on the same level), pointed to me, and said to the congregation, "That woman, my wife, has given me the best years of my life. She has stood by me in all my conflicts, all of my disappointments, and discouragements. She has also shared my success and I want you to know that she has been a good wife, a close friend and companion, and a good mother to my sons." The next

Sunday, after we arrived from church, he took his usual seat in the chair at the window. At 4 pm I heard an unnatural sound in his throat. I went to him—he was speechless and immediately I knew that he had suffered another stroke. I called to the boys, "Willard! Henry! Your father is ill again!"

The doctor came, ministered to him and said he would return later. When he returned, he told me, "Your husband may live a few hours, no longer."

It was night. I went outside my back door in the dark and there alone I wept bitterly. Regaining my composure, I went back into the room where Willard and I sat beside him during the twelve hours he lived. When he breathed his last, early in the morning of the 12th, it seemed that something left my body, beginning at the top of my head down through my feet through the floor. I could not cry. Never before had I understood the deep meaning of the word "bereaved." Poet's death left me desolate. It was as if I had lost an arm or a leg and been left helpless. Poet and I had been a team. We worked with and for each other. I helped him with his church work and he helped me with my work, whatever it might have been. We gave concerts together, Poet furnishing the literary selections from his own poems and stories, and I the piano numbers. Our concerts were always enjoyable and laughter-provoking, because of Poet's humor.

Whenever possible, we took our boys with us. They always enjoyed our presentations immensely. Many times they laughed, just at the wholehearted way the audience laughed. The next day, we would discuss the concert and all of us would express pride in each other. Now, all of this was ended. Poet was gone from us. No, I was not resentful towards God. It was just that I had lost my perspective. I was benumbed. I couldn't cry for relief. Ministers and other friends tried to console me, using the trite expressions of the day, but nothing said or touched me or appealed to me in any manner whatsoever. I was not frantic, but a deep sorrow froze me.

There were four colored churches in Westchester: the Presbyterian, the Baptist, and two branches of the Methodist church. Dr. Corrothers was the first minister to invite pastors of other denominations to preach in the Presbyterian church there. One of the pastors with whom he exchanged pulpits from time to time was Rev. Dunlap of the AME Church.[49] He and his wife had four sons. The three younger sons lived in the parsonage with their parents; the oldest son was married and lived in Connecticut. The Dunlap boys and

---

[49] According to the U.S. Census of 1910, the Rev. Coleman Dunlap (born circa 1861) and his wife Mahala (born circa 1866), both natives of South Carolina and living then in Harrisburg, had six children: Edward, James, Eunice, Cecil, Everett, and Harold.

our sons were very good friends. Many times pastors have had unexpected ministerial guests whom they were expected to house. When bedroom space was taxed, Mrs. Dunlap would call me, requesting me to let her sons sleep with ours for a night or two. When I found myself in a similar predicament, my boys would spend the night in the Methodist parsonage. So our two families were close.

Now, after Poet had been taken to Washington for burial in the old Harmony Cemetery and when Willard, Henry, and I returned to West Chester, I was still sorrowful. One day Mrs. Dunlap called me for a "heart to heart talk." She was disturbed about my continued lassitude, but she understood. She was a gentle lady, sweet and kind of manner—an altogether lovely woman. She had heard me say that I was willing to take care of Dr. Corrothers, no matter how long he had to sit in his chair by the window. She then related, "I had a daughter, a beautiful girl.[50]"I knew that must have been beautiful, for all her sons were such handsome boys. "She became ill and had to sit at the window. There she sat, suffering. She could do nothing, she could go nowhere. She saw her friends pass by, going to school, to church and to other activities, but there she sat. Her death broke my heart—I was crushed. Then I began to

---

[50] Eunice Dunlap was 15 in 1910.

think, 'How did *she* feel, sitting, sitting, sitting, year in and year out—what about *her*?' I asked myself. Now, Dr. Corrothers had been a strong man physically—an athlete, active in his church affairs, capable in literary pursuits, and then, suddenly, he was helpless. Yes, you were willing to nurse him 'no matter how long', but how do you think he'd feel, sitting, incapable of performing his usual pursuits? Mrs. Corrothers, *how about him*?" Mrs. Dunlap appealed to something deep within me. It was as if her spirit communed with my spirit. Out of the depths of her sorrow, she was able to help me with my sorrow. Without saying it in so many words, she showed me my selfishness in wanting Poet to live, no matter how much he suffered, physically and mentally. From that day I gained sufficient moral strength to begin to restore my composure. This happened sixty years ago, and today I thank Mrs. Dunlap (whether is on earth or in heaven I do not know), for that visit of spiritual comfort. She did for me what the ministers and other friends could not do. It was a lesson that I had to learn and that lesson I have never forgotten, through many heartbreaks later.

I received many letters from Dr. Corrothers' friends—writers, newspapermen of distinction, and other well-known personages from many areas of the country. One of the most moving tributes came from the NAACP's *Crisis* magazine, which editorialized in its April, 1917 issue:

"The death of James D. Corrothers, the poet, who died on Lincoln's Birthday, is a serious loss to the race and to literature. He was a man whom not only white people, but the colored people themselves did much to deprive of a real chance; yet he made his rugged way "in spite of the handicap", as his recent autobiography tells us."

Chapter X—A New Life

A few months after Poet died, I became ill and decided to go to Washington to be with Mom for a while. When I was better, I returned to West Chester. Everything was conducive to my remaining in the community permanently. Willard had been called into the service,[51] while Henry was still in high school. I was the organist of the church and had music pupils in the area and in Philadelphia. Moreover, as is the case of widows of Presbyterian ministers, I was given an annuity paid monthly. Then, too, West Chester was a beautiful city, not far from Cheyney and Downingtown, and it was a beautiful, scenic ride into Philadelphia, through fields of corn and dairy farms with their various breeds of cattle and their barns with their shining silos—all fascinatingly more beautiful at each season of the year.

The members of the church were intelligent, warm, and friendly and had very much endeared themselves to me. There was the Ganges family, which consisted of the parents,

---

[51] The draft registration of Willard D. Corrothers, dated June 5, 1917, reveals that he was living at 115 Holland Avenue in Ardmore, Pennsylvania and was working as a landscaper and gardener. Evidently he moved out of his stepmother's house within four months of his father's death.

two sons, and two daughters.[52] Mr. Ganges was a very successful ice cream manufacturer, who, according to the government inspectors, produced the purest ice cream around. After his death, his wife, son, and daughter-in-law took over the business. Even to this day, I still correspond with the daughter-in-law, Melba, and with the Ganges' last surviving daughter, Anna Johnson. Both have visited me in my home. Then there was the Curry family, whose daughter, Anne Spence, and her husband James, sang not only in the church choir, but in the special chorus I organized. Anne Spence sang the solo part in the "Inflammatus." Then there was John Connors, the principal of the high school, and his family. Wayne Cummings and his wife Elizabeth were dear friends, too. He was Methodist and she Catholic. Both have visited often and Elizabeth is still alive. While, in Washington, I had the necessity to have some dental work done by Dr. Clifford Frye, who was invited to dinner along with us. Dr. Frye was a trustee of the Fifteenth Street Presbyterian Church in Washington, and he talked freely about the church's problems, and Poet and I learned much. I

---

[52] On April 22, 1910, the U.S. Census shows the Ganges family living in West Goshen Township, Chester County, including George Ganges, age 73, a truck farmer, born in Pennsylvania, and his second wife, Alice, age 44, who was also a Pennsylvania native. They had been married for 26 years and had five children, four of whom were alive and residing with them: Herman, age 18; Roland, age 16; Anna, age 14; and Dorothy, age five.

had no way of knowing at the time that I would eventually become a member and the first woman officer in that congregation. There were many other friends in West Chester, and I had no intention of leaving. However, God had other plans. I became ill again and my mother persuaded me to move back to Washington.

"I think you ought to come back to Washington," Mom reiterated time and time again while I was home.

"No," I replied. "I want to stay in West Chester."

That fall of 1917, however, I became ill again and had to return home once again to be cared for by Mom. It now dawned on me that these repeated illnesses that forced me to return home were undoubtedly God's way of telling me that He wanted me in Washington, not West Chester. So, I gave in to Mom's counsel—and God's—and made my home with her and Marietta, who had recently obtained a divorce. Willard had married shortly after his father's death and soon after that had been drafted into the Army, so it was only Henry who accompanied me. He was enrolled in Dunbar High School.

Soon afterward, in December, I became violently ill. Henry was distraught. He was crying, repeatedly pleading, "Mom, please don't die! Please don't die!" I was rushed to Freedmen's Hospital in its new quarters on the north side of Bryant Street, between 4th and 5th.

For a long time I did not know what was wrong with me. Yet I had no fear, as I was confident that my life was secure in God's hands. Even though I knew that I was very, very ill, I somehow knew that I was not going to die. One day a fellow patient in the large ward where I was asked me, "When are you going to have your operation?"

"Operation?" I asked.

"Well," she said, "you wouldn't be on this ward if you weren't going to have an operation."

On January 2, 1918, the day I went into the operating room for major surgery, I was trembling visibly as Dr. Simeon Carson[53] spoke to me just as I was about to go under the ether. "How are you feelings?" he asked.

"I'm all right. I'm just a little shaky."

Dr. Carson smiled, "I see you can do the shimmy lying down." Then he became very serious. "Have you prayed?"

I told him that I had, and that I had no fear, but still I trembled until the anesthesia took effect. The operation was

---

[53] Simeon Carson (1882-1954) was a prominent Washington surgeon who operated a private hospital during the 20s and 30s a few blocks from Freedmen's. Mrs. Tucker said that Carson was then an assistant to Dr. LeCount Cook, an older surgeon (and son of the first pastor of Fifteenth Street Presbyterian Church).

a success and I grew stronger with every day.[54] Then came a terrible shock.

Henry came into the hospital room one day and quietly said that he had quit school and entered government work. His protests that he wanted to do service for his country and also help me financially did not really help me to overcome my shock and dismay, but I trusted that the Lord would make things right in His time and accomplish His will in spite of all.

In August, 1918 I was appointed to a position in the War Risk Division as a file clerk. And so I found myself in the "government service" so highly touted by Washington Negroes. For years I had heard of the inflated men in "government service." I was utterly shocked when I myself went to work for the government to find these workers were hauling furniture and cleaning out spittoons.

Later that summer I met an eighth grade classmate, Florence West, whom I had not seen in many years and who had since married a Pullman porter named William White. "Rose," she said to me, "Mr. White is away from home most of the time and I get so lonesome. What do you think of the idea of your living with me? Mr. White would desire it. He would feel so much more comfortable while he's away on

---

[54] Mrs. Tucker never identified her illness.

his runs, knowing that you, an old friend, would be there with me." Inasmuch as my sister and I got along best when not under the same roof, I consented, and made my home with the Whites. I found Mr. White to be a very fine man.

From time to time, friends would suggest that I marry again. In was initially offended at such thoughts. Within weeks of Poet's death, a minister had astounded me by saying, "Mrs. Corrothers, you should marry again. Marriage is a contract between two parties, a man and a woman. When one party to the contract dies, the contract is broken." On this basis, he urged me to remarry. I was astounded and insulted. But, by now I had grown used to the efforts of my friends to marry me off.

One night in September I answered the doorbell and a neatly attired man asked to see Mr. White. I asked him in and he went into the living room. He gave me his name, Tucker. I called to Mr. White, who had come in from his run earlier in the evening. He had eaten his dinner, bathed, and gone to bed. Mr. White asked me to ask Mr. Tucker to excuse him, as "he'll understand." I told Mr. Tucker this, we chatted a while, and then he left. When he visited another time, we were formally introduced. We met occasionally under similar circumstances and later I learned that he was asking questions about me. I soon began asking my friends about him. Their unanimous consensus was that he was a good, clean, honest man. When, shortly afterwards, he asked me to marry him, I was undecided. I had to do a great deal of thinking. Mr. Tucker was not a well-schooled man, which caused me to wonder if we had enough in common to make a success of our lives together. Then, too, I really did not know him that well. He was very quiet and really had not shared or confided very much in the time we had known each other. But my friends all insisted that I respond affirmatively to his proposal. And so I did.

Berthea Johnson Tucker was born in Amelia County, Virginia, on September 7, 1878.[55] I was always amused at his peculiar first name, which was a source of puzzlement to me until I learned that his parents were trying to spell "Berthier", but could not do so properly. Berthea's father was a carpenter who would go into the woods and cut down trees, dress the lumber, and build houses. He was often away from home for a week at a time. When weather permitted, he would sleep in the open and would study the moon, the stars, and the clouds. As a result, he became quite accurate in foretelling the weather. Berthea's mother, Mary

---

[55] The U.S. Census of 1880 shows Berthea Tucker, age 4, living in Bellefonte, Nottoway County, Virginia.
His father, Aaron Tucker, a carpenter, was then 62 years old. His mother, Mary, was 36. He had four siblings: Fannie, 16, William, 15, Indiana, 8, and Lottie, 2. Mary H. Tucker was evidently Aaron's second wife. By his first, he had a daughter Minerva (b. 1853) and a son Claiborne (b. 1855).

Johnson, was the typical country mother, who bore her husband four children, two boys and two girls.

During Reconstruction, many wealthy, dedicated Presbyterian woman from the North went to certain parts of Virginia and North Carolina and established schools for the children of former slaves, in which they themselves taught. It was at such a school that Berthea received his education. After his father died, he had to quit school. He had learned carpentry from his father, and when he came to Washington, he obtained work as a carpenter's helper. He had steady employment until he decided to go in the Pullman service to satisfy his longing to see different parts of the country. He became a skilled worker, and when the Broadway Limited, was inaugurated, no porter with under five years of service was assigned, and Berthea was among the first selected to serve on this new line.

I have heard porters say that he had the reputation of being the cleanest porter on the road. Often, because he look clean and fresh when he signed in at the yards, he would be signed out immediately without even being allowed to go home, because none of the incoming porters looked presentable. Berthea was assigned many times to special tours which lasted two or three weeks.

He was able to purchase a brick row house at 1828 7th Street, NE, where he lived with his mother and older sister

Indiana, or "Indy." Neither he nor his sister married, and Indy had died, in her 40s, shortly before I met Berthea.

Berthea was a slender man who said he was 5'8", although he did not look that tall. He had a dark brown complexion. He was a quiet, even at times, sullen man, and from the start, our marriage had problems. But these, I believe, were simply God's way of preparing me for the work that lay ahead.

It was a chilly evening when Mr. Tucker first took me to see his home on Seventh Street, N.E. I sat down while he went to the fireplace to make a fire. His mother, in her 80s, was in the same room and went upstairs without saying a word. I immediately sensed an overwhelming chilliness on her part. I asked Berthea about this and his response was, "Don't worry about her, Rose. All she has ever said to me about our plans is, 'I don't make marriages, so I ain't going to break any!'" He begged me not to let this influence me to change our plans.

When I told my son Henry about this, he warned me, "You're going to have trouble with the old lady." Nevertheless, despite my misgivings about her, Berthea Johnson Tucker and I were married on Thanksgiving eve, November 29, 1918 by the Rev. Luke Best, husband to my father's cousin, Mary Harvey. We had a small group of relatives and close friends in after the ceremony and all had an enjoyable time. Because of my son, I decided to hyphenate my surname, as Corrothers-Tucker.

Friday, the very next day, Berthea was due out and I went to my government job also. Saturday there was much to do to get things moving smoothly for me. Mother Tucker was that type of country folk who baked bread for every meal, and therefore what was left over was set aside. It was the accumulation of left-over foods that I had to clear away and other useless things which were in the way when I was in a hurry to get to work. Sunday I did not go to church but I arranged the kitchen so that articles I needed for the coming week would be easily accessible.

However, on Sunday Mother Tucker decided to become ill. When I went upstairs she had put her best sheets and spread on her bed; had put on a pretty nightgown, and there she lay ill. I prepared her breakfast, not letting her know that I was "on to her game." It was only just before the Christmas holidays that I attempted to make the house more homey. Whenever Berthea went out on his run, his mother would leave within the hour and visit her oldest son, Willie, and return just before Berthea was due home. In the bay window in the living room on a table was a large old-fashioned red lamp, which was an eye-sore. I placed it somewhere else. There was a table in the center of the living room upon which there were tintypes of Mother's relatives and friends, which I carefully wrapped and put away. I bought new draperies and lace curtains. When Mother Tucker returned from her visit to her son she saw the changes I had made. When I came home from work, she had changed them as she had them before. When this changing happened the second time, I explained to Berthea just what was being done, that it was child's play.

He told her very calmly that the house needed a younger touch, that he had told me to arrange everything as I saw fit. She became very angry and said many unkind things to him, whereupon Berthea took me from room to room (excepting her room), and asked me where I wanted this and that and he would place everything where I suggested and then he told his mother not to move them.

My marriage to Mr. Tucker had differences from the start. He was a very quiet man, and when we first met, I assumed that his silence was due to intellectual depth. But, after a short time, I learned that this was not the case. He seemed to have no depth at all. He was quite different from Dr. Corrothers, who was vivacious, open, and confiding in every matter. In contrast, Mr. Tucker tended to be grim and sullen, and, far from being confiding, it was usually impossible to know how he felt or what he was thinking. The difference between Berthea and Poet was very hard to adjust to. Being a Pullman porter, Mr. Tucker was away from home much of the time, and, at first, I looked forward to the times when he would be home. After a while, however, there were times when I was happier when he was on his runs. One just could not get him to talk; there seemed to be no way of penetrating the shell in which he had seemingly enclosed himself. Moreover, he seemed to have an inferiority complex. Not having had the opportunity for an extensive formal education, he seemed to resent my achievements. Whenever I had accomplished something, Poet had always commended me enthusiastically. But, whenever in later years I was cited for any achievement, Berthea, far from complimenting me or encouraging me, sulked and stewed, and would be untouchable and insufferable for days. If one tried to reason with him, he often fell into a towering rage.

He wanted to be head of the house. It was the custom in those days for the man to pay for the marriage license. One of Berthea's friends used to wave his marriage license in front of his wife and say, "Woman, I paid five dollars for you!" Sometimes I think that is how Berthea felt.

My marriage entailed other adjustments. I know that in most marriages, the wife has to make the adjustments, because the home activities revolve around the husband's work pattern. I had to leave the government service. Sometimes Berthea would come home from his run and have to leave while I was still at work. After this happened several times in succession, Berthea insisted that I should resign, for he said I was needed at home. I agreed with him. I had to give up my piano-playing. Whenever Berthea was home he said it bothered him, for he wanted to rest. Consequently, I was not able to practice sufficiently to maintain my former proficiency on that instrument.

I had to adjust to Berthea's being away from home so man days and at home for so many days. I learned his schedule rather quickly, and when he came home, his meals were always ready and the house was cleaned and inviting. Most of the time I took him to work and brought him home in the car. (He never learned how to drive). I had to adjust to Berthea's failure to encourage me for my efforts in the home, church, and community. I had to adjust to his lack of communication and his refusal to confide in me and his failure to share with me. I eased these encumbrances by prayer, patience, and several vacations without leaving the city.

My mother-in-law did not make things any better, either. Mary Johnson Tucker was a vicious, ignorant old woman who took a disliking to me from the start. When I was a little girl, some people kept vicious little black dogs called "feists." She reminded me of a feist. She began to tell people that I was not from Washington. "She came from

Philadelphia somewhere," she would tell her acquaintances. Among her own relatives in Virginia, she spread the story that I was "ugly, black, and as old as I am." When I had occasion to go to Amelia County in connection with the settlement of an estate in my husband's family and introduced myself to one of his relations, the man was incredulous. "You said you're *who*? You said you're *who*?" he repeated with disbelief. He and his relatives had heard old Mrs. Tucker's stories and were flabbergasted when they found out what I was really like!

My mother-in-law used to move her rocking chair to the doorway of her room, so as to better be able to pick up every detail of conversation that was going on in the house. Whenever the coal company would deliver our coal through the chute beneath the front window, Mother-in-Law would stand there with hands on hips, glaring at the coal man in tyrannical hauteur. One day the coal man came in and asked me, "Where is that old lady?" I had to tell him that she had died[56]. He reminisced how she used to stand at the window and scowl at him like a mediaeval queen, and we had a nice little laugh over her together. The poor old soul was irksome, but she could be funny, really!

---

[56] Mary Tucker does not appear with Berthea and Rosina in the 1920 census, so she must have died in 1919.

Chapter XI—The Washington Race Riot

In July, 1919, the summer after we were married, racial riots broke out here in Washington, DC. This was a real riot. Black soldiers had just come home from the war and demanded compensation and jobs. They stated that they had fought in the war and hundreds of their buddies had died for this country. Many were permanently crippled and compensation was due them. A tense and ugly mood prevailed. I do not know the one thing that sparked the conflagration, but before long, blacks and whites were fighting in the streets of Washington. During the day, all was peaceful, blacks and whites worked together side by side in their government and other jobs, but when night came, all hell broke loose. Every night there were fights and killings in the streets. These returned soldiers had learned war maneuvers in the Army and they put that knowledge to practice at that time. It was rumored that ammunition was relayed from as far away as New York City, then to Philadelphia, Baltimore, and then to Washington.

The rallying point for the blacks was the area around 6th Street, N.W., T Street, U Street, 7th Street, and all the area, including the Howard Theater. On the northwest corner of 7th and T was a men's clothing store called Brown's Corner, where on top of the building was stationed a machine gun and it was in that area that the blacks had their headquarters and set up a barricade. They were prepared to mow down any white mobs who intruded into the neighborhood. A barricade was established at 7th and M Streets, N.W., where whites dared not cross. This human barricade extended for many blocks—east, west, and north, to surround many of the black neighborhoods, around 7th Street, U Street, and Florida Avenue. Sixth Street was the center of the operation. Blacks from all sections of Washington engaged in protecting and supporting this human barricade and the blacks within the area. Women from Southwest's "Bloodfield" and "Hell's Bottom" overlooked the contempt previously shown them, and demanded their menfolk to go to Northwest Washington to "Protect the dicties." "Don't worry about us, " they said, "We can protect ourselves." Such black solidarity had never been known in Washington before. Over a period of two weeks or more dead bodies were found all over the city—mostly white. The city government was helpless—a white face dared no be seen in a Negro neighborhood after dark nor a black face in a white neighborhood. All who had firearms had cleaned and readied them for use if attacked.

Berthea was out of town at the time, but Henry was with me. We had some tense moments one night when we saw a convoy of armed white men ride down our street, four cars abreast. Why were they here? We were the only colored family in the neighborhood. Right in front of our house, one of the cars broke down. What would happen now? Supposing one of the hooligans should knock on our door, seeking assistance? And supposing he should discover us? I looked out the window again. However, the men made their own repairs, then moved on, without any trouble. That was our closest brush with danger at that time.

Mass meetings were held to advise citizenry as to what to do. I attended one such meeting at the Howard Theater, in which we were warned not to do anything unless attacked. Soon after that, government officials called a meeting for black professionals, ministers, doctors, school officials, and all well-known blacks and urged them to prevail upon "their people" to end the violence. Reverend Waldron[57], pastor of Shiloh Baptist Church, frequently passed for white when it would be to the advantage of his people. Having recently done this in order to ascertain the reactions and ideas of the white community, he vouched for the fact that the whites of Washington were now very much uneasy. Officials at the morgue would only let colored people look at colored corpses. Waldron, however, went to the morgue as was shown all the white and colored dead.

---

[57] The Rev. John Milton Waldron (1863-1931) was pastor of Shiloh Baptist from 1906 to 1929.

Most of bodies were white. He became aware of the fear the white citizens were suffering and reported it to the minister's association. Perhaps it was his report that convinced some of those who tended to encourage the rioting that they had made their point. At any rate, through the influence of black ministers, doctors, lawyers, and businessmen, the violence ceased.

Chapter XII—The Fifteenth Street Presbyterian Church

"Rosie, what church do you belong to now?" It was Sister Parker. I was standing in the vestibule of Second Baptist Church, where I had first come to know the Lord.

When I first returned to Washington, I began to attend services at the Fifteenth Street Presbyterian Church, then located at 15th and H Streets, N.W. The interior of the building was dark and gloomy, with dark, massive furniture, and dark, heavy stained glass windows. The people I knew found it uncongenial. Fifteenth Street Presbyterian Church was the only colored Presbyterian Church in Washington at that time, however, so I decided to visit my home church.

A member of Second Baptist., known as Sister Irving, whose daughter was baptized the same time I was, was so happy to see me enter the auditorium that in the middle of the service, she commenced to shout and scream. And when Sister Parker asked me what church I was now a member of, I told her, "Presbyterian." The creases of joy suddenly left her face. "Is it, Methodist?" As a child I instinctively felt that virtually the only way to God was through the Baptist Church. Methodists were tolerated, but Episcopalians, Presbyterians, and especially Catholics were regarded with consummate horror. When I told Sister Parker that I was not Methodist, her face became blank and she said no more. After worshiping at Second Baptist, I sadly concluded that I could never be comfortable there. Dr. Bishop Johnson had long since died. If I found the one church that seemed to be available uncongenial, well, perhaps God would bring about some changes. Who knows?

First known as the First Colored Presbyterian Church, Fifteenth Street was a very prestigious congregation. Founded in 1841 by John Francis Cook[58], a former slave, among its early pastors was Henry Highland Garnet[59], who was the first person of his race to deliver a prayer before Congress. Many of the most distinguished Negro citizens of Washington were members.

The members tended to be extremely color-conscious. Most of the members were Negroes so fair as to be easily mistaken for white. Many of these looked down on brown-skinned people. I remember a woman at the church who once sadly lamented, "I remember the time when you could sit at Fifteenth Street Church and look from the

---

[58] John Francis Cook (c.1810-1855) educator and pastor, also founded what became Metropolitan AME Church and Bethel Seminary, a school for black youth.

[59] Henry Highland Garnet (1815-1883), a former slave, an abolitionist and advocate of temperance, served as pastor of Fifteenth Street Presbyterian Church from 1864 to 1866.

balcony over all the congregation and not see one black face!" Because of this attitude, many of the members of Washington's growing colored community were repelled.[60]

But for many years fair skin and straight hair had been the ideal in beauty for many Washington Negroes. This, of course, was not universally true. Poet, my first husband, was very much opposed to this notion. He always said that there was a time when white people were ashamed of their color and would take the juice of a certain berry to apply it to their face to darken the skin. He also used to point out that the verse from the Song of Songs should read, "I am black *and* beautiful," rather than the usual translation, "I am black *but* beautiful." He pointed out that black people in the past had achieved much that their descendants could be proud of. Ethiopia was one of the first nations to become Christian. The eunuch to whom St. Philip preached brought the Gospel to the court of Queen Candace. Moses was instructed by the Egyptians in all the sciences. The Egyptians were certainly not white. Yet, the accomplishments of black and brown-skinned peoples of the

---

[60] Bernice Stewart House (1905-2008), granddaughter of a charter member of the church, recalled in an interview in 1999: "I don't think it's true that dark people weren't welcome, because I can remember that some of the elders...and ushers were brown skinned people. I mean *brown* (You didn't call anybody *black*. That was part of your family training!) There were not as many *very* dark people."

past was held from us at the time, He also pointed out that Negroes had many historical accomplishments of which they could be proud. When I was young, however, many colored people felt that they could have no self-esteem unless they made themselves as much like the white man as possible.

Times were changing, however. At the Howard Theater, where I often went for entertainment, there was one musical that I remember which struck me in that there were one or two numbers which exalted brown skin as a beautiful thing. Some of the expressions were "my satin-skinned brown," "my chocolate brown, my ebony sweetheart." Of course, in the present day this attitude has evolved to the point that "black is beautiful," but in those days many Washington Negroes were very much ashamed of their dark skin because they felt degraded because their skin was not white. When I came to be International Secretary-Treasurer of the Auxiliary to the Brotherhood, I had to deal with an official of the local Brotherhood whose skin coloring was almost white. There was a tendency for some others to look up to him as superior to the extent that he was able to influence them to do things which were undermining and should not have been done. It provoked me beyond words, so that I had some words with one of them who was under me at my office. "Oh, yes," I told him, "you do what Mars Charles tells you. That's Mars Charles speaking and you do just what he tells you whether it's right or wrong, whether you believe it or not!"

Such an attitude was displayed toward the Pastor of Fifteenth Street Presbyterian Church, Dr. Francis J. Grimke[61] He had been pastor for 40 years when I first met him and was by then quite old. A former slave, he was from a part of Charleston, South Carolina where the colored people were said to feel superior to everyone else. He was rather tall and very thin, and his skin coloring was white—absolutely white. There was no way of distinguishing his appearance from that of a white man. And it met members who revered him for no other expressed basis except that he was light with straight hair.

Dr. Grimke's sermons were very, very long and very intellectual. In fact, some of the members called them "essays." One member once remarked, "Dr. Grimke's so intelligent! His sermons are so intellectual that half the people don't even understand what they mean. Aren't we lucky to have so learned a man as pastor?" His sermons were indeed well-written and well-thought-out, but he *read* them, which was something I was unaccustomed to. He

---

[61] Francis James Grimke (1850-1937) was born in slavery in South Carolina, the son of his master. After graduating from Lincoln University and Princeton Theological Seminary, he served as Pastor of Fifteenth Street Church from 1878 until his death (except for a four years when he left to pastor a church in Jacksonville, Florida).

even read his prayers. His services were very staid and cold and formal.[62]

The thing that trouble me about Dr. Grimke, however, was that he appeared cold and unfeeling. He lost several good members through refusing to recommend their children to colleges. There was a little boy who had stolen something and gotten in trouble with the law. He was only about 10 or 12. Someone asked Dr. Grimke to speak for the child, but he sternly said, "He did it, didn't he? Well, then, just let him abide by the consequences." Now, I have known many times when Dr. Corrothers and I would go to court and plead for a child. There was a boy in our community who was put into our custody until his mother returned from work later in the day. So Dr. Grimke's attitude simply puzzled me.[63]

---

[62] Bernice House recalled that Fifteenth Street under Grimke was "different from churches....where the ministers must yell or walk or stomp or ask for a response. We had a very quiet, dignified service and intellectual messages. In that day, no one in the congregation made noise. That was completely out! It was a place of worship. You came in and sat down and got quiet and waited for the Scripture and the Message and the Music."

[63] Bernice House recalled Dr. Grimke as "a nice old grandfather type...He was quite interested in civil rights. He taught out of the Bible, but he was very interested in the life of the city. He was fair with grey hair and tall and stately. Everybody loved him. Billy Graham reminds me of him." She insisted that ministers of his generation were expected by their congregations to be dignified and reserved. C. Bernard Ruffin, Jr. (1914-1972) recalled Dr. Grimke as "very old and very reserved", but an elegant dresser, considered "one of the best-dressed men in

I had become a member in 1917. Soon after that, the congregation moved to the edifice at 15th and R Streets. The area where the old edifice stood was rapidly become commercial and the congregation was offered a handsome sum for the land on which the building stood. So they were paid enough to buy the vacant Christian Science Temple on the corner of 15th and R, then an all-white neighborhood, and they still had a goodly sum left over.

Soon after I joined the Fifteenth Street Presbyterian Church I was visited by a committee of the Elders who asked me to teach in the Sunday Church School. I said yes and Berthea had no objections. Among the teachers I met was Miss Elizabeth Bamfield, who later married Woolsey Hall, a well-known native Washingtonian. I was certain that Mrs. Hall was a member of long standing in the church, but when comparing dates years later, we discovered that while I joined the church two or more years before she left South Carolina to take a position in the Federal Government, she had begun teaching before I had. Mrs. Hall and I took our

---

Washington." He said the typical theme of Dr. Grimke's sermons was, "If you sin and don't repent, you're going to hell and burn up." He said Grimke would "shout at the top of his feeble voice and shake his feeble fist." The Rev. Robert Pierre Johnson (1914-1974), pastor of Fifteenth Street between 1954 and 1967, told the following Dr. Grimke story: "There was a prominent physician, Dr. Ware, who was a member of the church, whose son committed suicide. When the physician asked Grimke to conduct his son's funeral, Grimke refused, saying, "No. He's in hell."

teaching assignment very seriously. One concern of the teachers was how to keep students in their classes as they grew older. We discerned a gradual decline in their attendance on entering high school; that there was a decided loss when entering college and the trend was worsened after leaving college. Oh, the joy we experienced when these young people, after marrying, brought their children in the Sunday School for Christian training! Mrs. Hall has since died. I miss her very much, for she worked with me many years at training children in spiritual living. I am now the last living teacher who taught through the years and I thank God as I sit in my pew Sunday mornings and note these students, now grown, serving as elders, trustees, deacons, teachers, superintendents, singers in the church choir, heads of important committees and others good substantial supporters of all activities—social, spiritual, and financial interests of the church fellowship.

Many Presbyterians were turned away from the Fifteenth Street Presbyterian Church by the attitude of some of its members; thus many coming from other cities joined other denominations here. This caused an immeasurable loss of potential membership for the church.

About 1921 I was visited by the Rev. John W. Lee of Philadelphia, the good friend of my first husband who had conducted the services and preached the funeral sermon. He said, "Mrs. Tucker, I am here to set up a new church. The Presbytery feels that Fifteenth Street has been derelict in evangelizing the city, so they sent me here to set up a mission, if I can find sufficient support. I thought that maybe you could help me establish a mission."

The services were held in Moses Hall on Barry Place, N.W., one of the short streets just off Georgia Avenue. On this particular street were several small halls where secret benevolent societies, such as the "Moses", "Galilean Fishermen" and others held their business meetings. As Dr. Lee visited Presbyterians who had no church home, he heard such comments as, "I don't feel wanted at Fifteenth Street Church; the members are snobbish." Many of these people from various cities were prominent members in their home churches and they were offended by this attitude and this lack of Christian fellowship. However, through the influence of Dr. Lee, many of these disaffected people gladly joined the mission and were able, within a short time, to work up a goodly membership. I assisted Dr. Lee further by playing the organ and leading the singing at the Sunday night services.

Within about three years the mission was ready for a permanent building, having moved in the meantime from Barry Place to the 12th Street YMCA to accommodate the increased attendance. The Washington Presbytery sent a commissioner to a congregational meeting at Fifteenth Street Church, who said, "Now we, the Presbytery, *can* supply the money to erect an edifice, but we feel this would be the proper thing for *you* to do." After an intelligible discussion, I observed, "For us to provide the necessary funds for this project would be the greatest act of missionary work that this church could possibly be permitted to do." I motioned that the sum of $12,000 be given for this purpose.[64] The motion passed. The mission became Tabor Presbyterian Church, which flourished for more than 50 years on the corner of 2nd and S Streets, N.W. It was a large and vital congregation. When it closed its doors and merged with a white congregation, I was left with a sense of disappointment and grief. Yet I am happy to have been a party to the organization of this church that served God's purpose so well in its time.

Dr. Grimke, the Pastor of Fifteenth Street Church, stated about 1924 that he was no longer able to continue the pastorate of the church, and so the task of finding a successor began. Among three candidates who spoke at our church was Dr. Halley B. Taylor, whose pastorate was at Paterson, New Jersey. Dr. Grimke liked him and insisted that he be brought here *"under any circumstances."*

---

[64] This was from the sum left over from the sale of the old building.

Salary was the problem. Dr. Taylor had a wife and several young children and could not exist on the salary which Fifteenth Street was paying Grimke [65] at the time. Affluent doctors, lawyers, teachers and others were contributing for themselves and their spouses 12 dollars per year—25 cents per Sunday.

Now it was apparent that a much higher salary would have to be offered Dr. Taylor. The higher salary was agreed upon, and at Dr. Grimke's active insistence, Dr. Taylor came to us.[66] His status was that of "Associate Pastor", which left Dr. Grimke in control and Dr. Taylor could do little on his own initiative. Dr. Taylor felt that it was part of his duties to visit the members, but was informed by the officers of the church that he was not to visit any member unless invited. And yet there were those who condemned him for not visiting. As an officer in the church, I called on a sick member one day who lived in a third floor apartment in a doctor's home. After waiting an interminable length of time,

---

[65] Grimke was a childless widower.

[66] Halley Blanton Taylor (1879-1965), a native of New Bern, North Carolina and a graduate of the college and seminary of what became Johnson C. Smith University, carried the title of Associate Pastor from June, 1925 until Dr. Grimke's death in 1937, although he assumed almost all pastoral responsibilities. C. Bernard Ruffin, Jr. recalled that Grimke's role after that was limited to the delivery of a sermon every fourth Sunday until, in his last years, he was too ill to preach at all.

I was ushered into her bedroom and was greeted with, "Oh, it's you, Mrs. Tucker. I was afraid it was one of my school parents. You know how they are. They come in and sit and sit. Reverend Taylor was here to see me the other day, but I sent word that I was too ill to see him." I have always believed that during grave illnesses the minister, next to the doctor, is privileged to visit the patient at any time. Moreover, there were those who were not reconciled to Dr. Grimke's relinquishment of the full pastorate and others who gave Dr. Taylor their full support. And so a split occurred among the members of the church with one group favoring Dr. Taylor and the other Dr. Grimke.

October was the month of the year when members of the congregation were returning from their vacations. It was called "Rally Month". It was not a fund-raising rally, but a rallying of the organizations of the church. Dr. Grimke preached the entire four straight Sundays in the month. I sincerely hoped that in at least one of his sermons he would say something in support of Dr. Taylor and thus ameliorate the situation, but on the first Sunday in October, he said nothing about it, nor did he on the second or third Sunday. Growing very concerned, I decided to have a talk with Dr. Grimke.

This was quite a task, as Dr. Grimke was not easily approached. I had to pray over the matter. I prayed expressly over this matter from that Sunday (the third in the month) every day until Friday, until I could muster enough courage to discuss my concern with him. Friday I went to his home. "Dr. Grimke," I said, "I had expected you to say something to ease the tension which has developed in our church. I had hoped that you would say something to unite the officers and members of our church; and I hoped you would say something to support Dr. Taylor and the duty of the members toward him.

There was an agonizing silent as Dr. Grimke gazed stone-faced at me with his cold blue eyes. Then, with quiet coldness, he emotionlessly said, "Mr. Taylor ought to leave. He should go."

"Do you mean Dr. Taylor should just get up and move out?"

"Yes. The people do not like his ministry."

"But the church engaged him and it was you, Dr. Grimke, it was you who told the commissioners to 'bring him under any circumstances.'"

Without changing his expression, Dr. Grimke quietly replied, "They do not like his ministry."

I no longer remember what my reply to him was, but when I left Dr. Grimke, I was distressed and grieved at his insensitivity and unchristian attitude toward Dr. Taylor, a brother minister whom he himself had urged to accept the pastorate of the congregation.

Soon afterwards, however, Dr. Grimke retired altogether from active ministry and Dr. Taylor became pastor in fact[67] and, now that he was uninhibited in his work, he soon won the hearts of the membership and the respect of the community in general.

The congregation, however, was not in the habit of supporting the church financially, and for the minister and for need improvements in the building, the trustees asked me to conduct a financial rally. On the designated Sunday morning for my appeal, I went to the front of the church and talked about money. This was contrary to the tradition of the congregation. I called the attention of the people to a spot in the ceiling where the rain had come in and said, "You're a dignified church. Doesn't it reflect on your dignity when you look upon that damp spot? Doesn't it offend you not to pay your pastor's salary? Now, I want each of you, every member of this church, *right now* to pledge 10 dollars. I do not want Dr. and Mrs. to pledge 10 dollars, but each Doctor $10 and each Mrs. $10; not Professor and Mrs. $10, but I want each member of this church to give $10. State your name as you rise, so that Mrs. Handy may record it. Names

---

[67] Although Taylor became pastor in fact, he remained "Associate Pastor" until Grimke died.

were called from every section of the church. Names were called from every section of the church. Dr. Wilder, Senior, who was not a member, pledged $25 for his wife, who was. Over $800.00 was pledged that morning, the largest amount ever promised in the long history of Fifteenth Street Church. Many seemed to feel proud of themselves, but, before I returned to my pew, I said to them, "I thank you, but a little Baptist church with 40 members would have done better than that!" But they made good on their pledges and Dr. Taylor was very, very pleased.

As time went on and Dr. Taylor's ministry progressed, many changes were made. Most of the older trouble-makers died off. Many people came in from different presbyteries and different backgrounds. Many things were done differently. When I first came to Fifteenth Street, many of the members of the church considered it demeaning to be seen in the kitchen and would not even provide their services for church dinners. I have lived to see a complete change; I have lived to see members willingly lend a helping hand in all the church's activities. It is no longer necessary to hire cooks for church dinners.

I can recall a particular member who first gave me the cold shoulder. This became apparent when I visited Mrs. Boyce, the head of the local chapter of the YWCA, who was ill at the time. By then I was the first woman Trustee and thought I should visit her. While I was there, the member whom I just mentioned appeared.[68] She said nothing, but her attitude clearly expressed what she would probably have liked to say: "What are *you* doing here?" Although Mrs. Boyce was quite congenial, her visitor was openly disdainful of me. She was of the social set and the wife of a prominent doctor. They had a large gracious home. Years passed and the doctor's widow fell on hard times. Her husband died and she and her daughter were forced to leave their beautiful home and live with a son. In time, the once-proud lady lost her sight and became hard of hearing. On the day that I was hostess at the monthly meeting and luncheon for our Senior Citizens' group, the Leisure Golden Age Club, in attendance was the sister of the doctor's widow. I happened to be serving the sandwiches and, during the course of the affair, the sister said, "Mrs. Tucker, I'm not going to eat my sandwich. I'm going to take it to my sister."

I told her, "Oh, you eat it. I'll give you some to take to your sister." So I sent the sister some sandwiches and cake. Immediately, I got notes not only from the sister but from the mother and daughter as well, expressing profuse thanks. Ever after that, the family was very appreciative. Whenever I came with my pastor to serve Communion, the

---

[68] Violet B. Warfield (1868-1963), wife of Dr. William Alonza Warfield

doctor's widow was glad to have me in her home. Now her daughter[69] is in the nursing home and comes to church when someone brings her. She will not leave the church without speaking to me. One day they were about to put her in the car when she declared, "No, I'm not going before I speak to Mrs. Tucker!"

I became a trustee—the very first woman officer in the history of our church, and a few years later the chairman of the board. During this time I was voted an elder, and served many years.

About two weeks after my son Henry died[70], a teacher in the Sunday School, Mrs. Mollie Barrier, asked for an appointment and when she arrived at my home, she expressed her sorrow at my son's death and waited until she was sure that I was more reconciled to his loss. She said that after had lost her husband, she desired to do something constructive—preferably to teach in the Sunday School. She recounted to me that she had been undecided because of the adverse attitude of one of the officials when she consulted her about her desire to teach. She went to the Sunday School session, but decided to make her final decision depending upon how well she was received. When she entered the

---

[69] Violet B. Warfield, Jr. (1902-1985)

[70] This would have been May, 1945

room, I met her, introduced myself and then introduced her to the other teachers. "Your friendliness and the cordial reception of the other teachers caused me to decide to teach and ignore the previous affronts. Mrs. Tucker, I came here to tell you this, for otherwise you might never know what influence you had in this part of my spiritual life." Mrs. Barrier had a class of 15 boys, all of whom but one joined the church.

Many have attributed their decision to become members of Fifteenth Street to me. "You know, Mrs. Tucker likes everybody," someone said in my hearing. "She put her arm around you." All I can say is that if I have been permitted to do any good through the church I have served over the years as a Sunday School teacher, Trustee, and Ruling Elder, it is through Christ and His will that I have made the effort.

Chapter XII-The Brotherhood of Sleeping Car Porters

After Mr. Tucker and I were married, I came to know several Pullman porters and their wives. One of Berthea's best friends was a porter by the name of John Morrison, who, with his wife, came frequently to our home to play cards. On one visit in 1925, Mr. Morrison told us that a man named Ashley Totten and two or three Pullman porters in New York were trying to start a union. Mr. Morrison urged my husband to join and bade me encourage him to do so. I soon became interested in the Pullman porters and their cause.

In 1925, the Pullman Company employed about 6000 porters, maids, and other attendants on their railroad sleeping cars. These people worked under horrific conditions. They were virtual slaves to the Pullman Company. The porter had a car assigned to him and he would have to take care of that car. He had to open the beds when the occupants of the car were ready for them, and he had to straighten out the covers and blankets. It was a picture, the way they folded those blankets and arranged those pillows in the berths! That was quite a job, going from one end of the car to the other, opening up the beds on both sides, fixing up the beds where the seats were, preparing the towels and soap and everything, right there on the spot.

The Pullman porter was dependable and trustworthy. In fact, he was truly an asset to the Pullman Company, for it was the porter's service that was sold to the traveling public. It was traditional for a wealthy white husband to take his wife to the railroad station and place her in the care of the porter, or a father to place a small son or daughter in his care, for it was known that they would be taken care of during the trip and gotten off at the right stop. Because of his contacts, the porter was able to direct black passengers to hotels or rooming houses in cities en route that would accommodate them. Also, because of his contacts with wealthy and high-ranking passengers, the porter acquired a bearing, dignity, and culture.

Despite all this the porters were ill-paid. They were treated like slaves, as part of the equipment. He had to abide by over 200 rules. In 1916, the porters' wages were only $48.00 per month, which was very low, even for those days. By 1925, the wage had increased to $72.50 per month, but still that was scarcely enough to live on. Many of the porters had large families to support. They had to depend on tips. Many of the passengers would, however, tip handsomely. Some would give them several dollars, even as much as $10, for going to the dining room and bringing them their meals. But some did not give much, and porters could not depend on tips for their living. Then, too, the porter had to pay for any breakage in the passenger's baggage. They had to clean shoes, but they had to furnish their own blacking and their own cloths. Anybody on the train could complain about them, and, if they did, the porter would be in trouble, for the passenger's word was always taken above that of the porter. There was no limit to the hours the porters had to work. They had no provisions for sleeping, and when they were not actually working, they had to sit in the aisle where they were constantly subjected to drafts. As a result, nearly all Pullman porters seemed to have chronic respiratory problems. Their eating facilities were poor, and they sometimes had to do without food for long periods of time. As a result, many porters developed digestive diseases.

Since 1910, attempts had been made to organize a union, but these had failed because of the Pullman Company's spy system. By means of "stool pigeons"—porters who were bribed or lured by promises of favor or advancement into collusion with the management—the Company learned the names of the porters who were trying to organize. These men were publicly exposed and ridiculed, or fired, or both. As a result, many porters were afraid to go to organizational meetings, and with good reason. They had families to support and wanted to keep their jobs, even with low wages and poor working conditions. A bad job was better than none at all.

To make things worse, the Pullman Company set up its own "company union" in 1920, which they claimed represented the men. However, the "yellow dog" contracts[71] which they offered did not improve conditions much. Moreover, the management used the company union as a home base for the porters who were loyal to the company and acted the part of "stool pigeons" against those who were union-minded.

When in 1925 another attempt to form a union, nosed out by the company "stool pigeons", ended with the firing of the instigators, the porters decided that they had to look for a leader who was not affiliated with the Pullman Company and who was therefore beyond the company's reach. A. Philip Randolph was an editor who had taken the side of the porters and raked the Pullman Company over the coals in the columns of his magazine, *The Messenger*. Some of the leaders of the union movement had heard Mr. Randolph speaking and asked him whether he would take over the leadership of the embryonic union. He said that he would, and that was when the Pullman porters' union really got started—the Brotherhood of Sleeping Car Porters, as it was named.

---

[71] A contract in which an employee agrees not to join a labor union.

In the third chapter of the Book of Ezekiel, the prophet relates, "I came to them of the captivity at Telabib, that dwelt by the river Chebar, and I sat where they sat, and remained there astonished among them for seven days. And it came to pass at the end of the seven days, that the word of the Lord came unto me, saying, 'Son of man, I have made thee a watchman unto the House of Israel.'" God sent Ezekiel to abide with the captives from Israel for seven days. In so doing, Ezekiel became acquainted with their problems. He sat where they sat and learned what slavery had done to them. He sat where they sat and learned that they were poor, heavy-laden, sorrowful, and oppressed. He sat where they sat and learned of their every-day existence. He advised them, admonished them, comforted them, loved them. He understood their desire for a better existence. When he learned all that God would have him learn, God made Ezekiel a watchman over them to guide them as God would have him.

Mr. Randolph was like the Prophet Ezekiel. The Pullman porters were captives. They worked long hours and their pay was negligible. The company controlled them, for when they left home for the sign-out office, they never knew if they would be allowed to go out on their lines or not, or, when their check was received, they often found that deductions were made for breakage or losses. The sign-out office knew the private affairs of practically every porter, for the company-informer-porter provided them with it.

But a good man came to the Pullman porters. He sat where they sat on the banks of the Harlem River. He sat where they sat. He sat down with the porters and heard their story. He ate with them, slept with the, suffered with them, and learned in detail their problems. He sat where they sat and learned that they were poorly paid and overburdened with work, discouraged, and oppressed. He learned what it meant to be a Pullman porter. He advised them, he admonished them, he comforted them, he loved them. He understood their desire for a better existence. Then God put it in his heart to say, "I will be a watchman over you." Thus, through the efforts of A. Philip Randolph, the Brotherhood of Sleeping Car Porters was born.

I helped to form the branch in Washington. I think they'll say I was the most active leader in its genesis.

I attended the organizational meeting of the Washington Division of the Brotherhood. It was in the John Wesley Church, and Mr. Randolph, International President, and Mr. Ashley Totten, the International Secretary-Treasurer, had charge of the meeting and spoke. The auditorium was crowded with porters, but not all of them were friendly. Many of those in attendance were "stool pigeons" who informed the Pullman officials of those porters who seemed to be active in the new union. These men were company pets, who, for their efforts, obtained the best runs. They were allowed to bump porters on the same line when they thought that one car yielded more tips than the one the other was on. One such man sat beside me and asked me to help him obtain the names of those porters who seemed to be sympathetic to the union.

"Help you! For what?" I said indignantly.

At various points in Mr. Randolph's talk, I asked him, "Do you object to that?" He did not answer. He had come down to take the names of the participants and wanted me to help him. Of course, I vehemently refused. Wisely, Mr. Randolph did not ask any of the porters to speak, so as to give the "stool pigeons" no opportunity to learn with any degree of certainty the identity of the porters who were active. He and Mr. Totten did all the talking, explaining what should be done. The men got a good idea of the mechanics of the union and what was needed in order to put it into operation.

So, the Washington branch of the Brotherhood was organized. The president was a Mr. McClellan, but I can't think of this first name.

Much more had to be done in the way of organizing the Washington Division. Information and directives had to be relayed between Mr. Randolph in New York and the porters in Washington. Public meetings were out of the question. Any overt involvement by anyone employed by the Pullman Company was suicide. So, it devolved upon the wives of the porters to do most of the organizational work.

Fortunately, most of the porters, or so it seemed, had very fine wives who were dedicated as much or more than their husbands to the formation of the union. I was asked to act as a liaison between Mr. Randolph and the Washington Division. Material was sent to me and I myself would disseminate it to the men. I kept them in touch with what was going on, because it was dangerous for them to let it be known, even to each other, that they were members. One never knew for sure who and where the informers were. I collected dues and sent them on to New York. I visited the families of the porters and personally explained to them what the union meant and what benefits it would bring. I suppose I visited over three hundred porters in Washington, telling them the advantage of their being members, and letting them know just what progress was being made, what difficulties were being encountered, and how the other men were responding. There were some men who were willing to join the organization but who were prevented from doing so by their apprehensive wives. On the other hand, there were many men whose wives were eager for them to join, but who balked for fear of losing their jobs. There were some women who put their husband's names on the rolls and paid their dues. If I dare say so, it was the women who made the union in the early days. The men were afraid, though with good reason.

Opposition grew stiff. As the union continued to grow, so grew in vehemence the efforts on the part of the Pullman Company to squelch it. By means of their informers, who were invariably rewarded with supervisory positions, they stepped up their efforts to fire any porters suspected of association with the Brotherhood. The white Pullman conductors opposed us. So did many "Big Niggers." I remember one pompous Methodist bishop who observed, "Dese men, dey got good jobs, and now you gonna fix it so dey not gonna have no jobs at all!" We had trouble with at least one other civil rights organization, which I shall not name, to the point that Mr. Randolph threatened to sue them.

But we had friends. Dr. Taylor, who had recently come to Washington, supported our cause wholeheartedly and permitted us to hold meetings at church. The Rev. Arthur Elms, pastor of the People's Congregational Church, then located at 7th and M Streets, N.W., was also friendly and allowed us to meet at times in his church. We likewise occasionally had mass meetings at the Florida Avenue Baptist Church.

Most meetings, however, were held at my own home on 7th Street, N.E. I had to close the blinds and all the doors. When the International officers came, they usually stayed right in my home. Mr. Randolph lodged with us more than once.

Still, many porters balked. They did not understand the advantages it meant for them. They still wanted to play the role of "white folks' nigger." When I urged them to join, they would tell me, "No, we're going to stand in with the white men and work against this thing." I had a very dear friend who wanted so very much for her husband to be in the union, but he was a company man and refused to join. He and others opposed the union, believing that this course of action was to their benefit. They were sure that we could never break the system. "The Pullman Company will *never* sit across the table with Mr. Randolph," they said.

Through their informers, the Pullman Company in Washington learned that I was instrumental in organizing the Washington Division of the Brotherhood. One day my husband Berthea, who was a porter in regular service, went to work and returned shortly afterwards, explaining that he was not permitted to go out. He had been put on the "Extra Board." He told me that the sign-out man at the yards had told him, "There's nothing that could take you off your job, nothing in hell, but your wife's activities in the Brotherhood of Sleeping Car Porters!"

I got to thinking over it and said to myself, "Now, I'm not going to take that. I'm going to the office and see the superintendent."

The men at the yard knew all about me. Through their informers, they knew that Mr. Tucker and I owned a house, they knew that I had a piano, and they knew that I had a son who was in college. So, anyway, I called the superintendent.

"I'm Mrs. B.J. Tucker."

The man who answered said, "Wait a minute," and somebody else came to the phone. This second man told me that the superintendent was "in conference." Now I knew that it was the superintendent to whom I had first spoken, and when I mentioned that I was Mrs. B.J. Tucker, he skipped. I called later on and got once again the response that the superintendent was "in conference." The next morning I called once more and again was told the same thing.

So I went to Union Station and found the superintendent's office. When I was told that he was still "in conference," I went in the room downstairs in the station and wrote a note, asking a red cap if he could take it up to the

Pullman office. He returned, saying that the superintendent was "in conference."

I was very unhappy. I called a Brother Massey, a porter and a very fine union man. I told him what happened. He said, "You go back and see the man *over* the superintendent. You tell him that you'll take it to Chicago [the headquarters of the Pullman Company] if he doesn't see you."

I went back over to the station and went to the office of the man who was over the superintendent. As a rule, there was a girl sitting at the desk at the door, but at that particular moment she was not there. I saw a man walking up and down as if he was doing some serious thinking. I asked if he could be the man I was seeking, naming his name. He said, "Yes," and, as he answered me, he walked into his office, which was in the next room, and I followed him in there. I said I came to see about my husband, Mr. B.J. Tucker.

"What about him?" the official asked.

I said that he was taken off his run and I said, "John Hammond, the sign-out man, told my husband that 'nothing in hell could take you off that run except your wife's activities in the Brotherhood of Sleeping-Car porters.' I pounded on his desk and said, 'I want to tell you that nobody has anything to do with what I do! You hired my husband. You didn't hire me!'"

He said to me, "So, why are you taking the matter up?"

"Because," I replied, "they brought me in to it." Then I added, "Now, you take care of this matter, or else I'll be back!"

He was so surprised he didn't know what to do. Here was this nigger woman coming here and acting like that. The other people had been afraid. Other women had gone there, begging, "Please put my husband back on the run," but here I went there banging on his desk. Well, you know, for a black woman to speak up to a white man like that in the 1920s was extraordinary. Naturally, he thought that there was a powerful somebody supporting me.

Mr. Tucker got his run back.

The Pullman Company continued its intimidation, but we did not give up. *The Black Worker,* the Brotherhood's house organ, wrote in January, 1957, that during the late 1920s, when the workers in Washington were being severely harassed, "For quite a period, only the voice of Sister Tucker could be heard, pleading the cause of the Brotherhood. She went up and down the streets of Washington and into the offices of the Washington Pullman superintendent and courageously spoke her piece about the right of the porters to join the Brotherhood."

So we got the union together, got it organized, but we had to go through many difficulties. We had to go to the Interstate Commerce Commission, we had to go before various Senate Committees, but finally were able to get some results.

In 1929 the Brotherhood was granted a federal charter by the American Federation of Labor. In 1934, however, Congress passed the Railway Labor Act, which gave employees the right to organize and bargain collectively through representatives of their own choosing. The Pullman Company, however, refused to recognize the Brotherhood as a bargaining agent for its porters. The next year, through the influence of Mr. Randolph, the act was amended to cover porters, who were specifically classified as railroad workers, who were now entitled to all the benefits of the act.

Despite the pessimism of the porters who insisted that the Pullman Company would never sit across the table to bargain with Brother Randolph, in 1937 the Company did in fact bargain with him and with other Brotherhood officials and the first agreement was signed, which raised the minimum wage from $77.50 to $113.00 per month and cut the hours of work from 400 per month to 240. After that, increases were steady. Working conditions improved dramatically. Employees gained the right not to be "disciplined, suspended, or discharged without a hearing." We were given the right to select representatives, to produce and question witnesses, and to have transcripts of the hearings. We had a right to appeal to the National Railroad Adjustment Board. All these things had been denied porters before. We were the first Negro labor organization to be officially recognized in the world.

For the "stool pigeons," it was a world turned upside down. Many of these men had fought the union, thinking that they had an "in" with the Company and that they had special privileges. Now they found that the union men were benefitting.

One of them did not work one day and an official asked him why. "Well, I was out there, looking after some of this stuff for the Company."

The Pullman Company official told him, "Now, listen. You may as well join the union. You have to join it or else you can't work." So, that was the way it was. After the union came into being, one had to abide by the shop agreement or lose the job. One may think that some of these union men were drastic in their actions, but the men of the Brotherhood sacrificed a great deal for their union and did not want to see somebody come and break it up. You could start a small war knocking the Brotherhood.

Chapter XIV-The Ladies' Auxiliary

At the same time that we were trying to organize the men, we were also organizing the porters' wives. When the International Ladies' Auxiliary was finally organized officially in 1938, it marked the culmination of thirteen years of struggle. A labor union is not only for the men, but also for their wives and families. For instance, in the event of a strike, the wife must understand why her husband is striking and she must support him so that there will be a solid phalanx against the opposition. It was absolutely necessary, I felt, that the Pullman porters' wives be cognizant of their husband's working conditions. The porter's home had to be a union home. Without a union home, the porter could not be a good union man. I said this many times, all over the country.

We really had a ladies' auxiliary before we had a Brotherhood. As I said earlier, it was really the women who were instrumental in forming that organization. The men were often afraid and it was their wives who did the organizing. Accordingly, very early, women's councils were formed. These sprang up rapidly all over the country, especially in the West. There women had suffrage long before our eastern women, and they were more used to political matters there, and, as a result, they were particularly strong. It was harder to organize the women back East, but we finally succeeded. The Washington local was organized by me in my home on 7th Street. By the late 1930s, there were local councils in Washington, New York, Chicago, Denver, Cleveland, and most of the other great railroad centers in the United States and Canada—42 in all.

In 1938 Brother Randolph called a convention of the women in Chicago. He requested all the heads of the local councils to be present, as he wanted these 42 bodies to unite into an International Auxiliary (U.S. and Canada) which would have its own President and Secretary-Treasurer and other officers, just as the porters did. Mr. Randolph insisted that I attend. At that time, I had no means of getting to Chicago, so Mr. Randolph telegraphed me: "Sister Tucker, I understand that you do not have transportation and maintenance to Chicago. We need your presence. We need your counsel. It is the duty of the Ladies' Auxiliary to see that you get to Chicago. If they cannot do it, the Brotherhood will. If they cannot do it, call me at once and we will send you what is necessary." The matter was taken up by my local and the Washington Auxiliary sent me.

The convention met on September 24, 1938. Mary McLeod Bethune, the famed educator and founder of Bethune-Cookman College in Florida, was the guest speaker at the rally. It was the first time I had ever seen Mrs.

Bethune and I was very impressed. She was, shall we say, physically quite unprepossessing[72], but when she spoke, she reflected a truly beautiful woman. In later years I met her when I represented the Brotherhood at her birthday celebration at the Howard Theater here in Washington, DC. In private conversation, she was a kind, warm, engaging, and altogether a lovely person.

When the Auxiliary got down to the business of the convention, Mr. Randolph announced publicly that he was appointing Sister Tucker chairman of the Constitution and Resolution Committee. It was an important and difficult assignment. It was *the* committee to lay the very foundation of the organization. Mr. Randolph suggested that when all the other committees completed their work, they should come into the session and observe the proceedings of my committee. As suggested, in time, all delegates were in the assembly hall to listen to our proceedings on occasion—observing the birth of the first international labor organization of black women in the world.

It took me a full day to read and explain every resolution before a vote was taken on each recommendation. Then we took a half of the next day to place the report before

---

[72] Mary McLeod Bethune (1875-1955), educator, civil rights leader, and advisor to the Roosevelts. Off the record, Mrs. Tucker described Mrs. Bethune as extremely ugly.

the full convention. When I arrived in Chicago for the convention, I had no idea what Mr. Randolph's organizational plans were and therefore, I was amazed at the manner some of the delegates and their friends campaigned for offices, really beginning with the very first day of the convention, though the election for the permanent offices was not until the last day.

The President of the Chicago Auxiliary, Mrs. Halena Wilson[73], was running for the presidency of the International Auxiliary, and while her own auxiliary had only three delegates, the local members visited the open sessions and circulated among the delegates, saying, "Vote for Sister Wilson for president." There were those campaigning for other offices, too. Their action was, to say the least, "vigorous." The campaign amused me at first, but later it disturbed me, for delegates were accosted in every conceivable place and at every conceivable time. I was alone. I knew no one, really. I had met Sister Lassiter, president of the New York council, once at a zone conference in New York. But I knew none of the delegates and I sought no office.

When the balloting was over, Sister Wilson won the presidency. She began to preside immediately, as the

---

[73] Halena Wilson (1895-1975) was the president of the Chicago Auxiliary.

balloting for the other officers continued. After a while, it was brought to my attention by a lady who was sitting on the opposite side of the room from me that each time balloting was done, someone from the back came to the president and requested voting instructions for each ballot. At first I did not believe it, but sure enough, on the next ballot, someone came from the rear of the hall for instructions from Mrs. Wilson as to how to vote. I objected, and took th floor. "Madame President," I said, "don't you know you are doing wrong, telling delegates how to vote?"

Mr. Randolph, Mr. Totten, Mr. Webster, and all the other big international men were there, and poor Mrs. Wilson was quite embarrassed.

"I beg your pardon," she said weakly.

When we got finished, I was elected International Secretary-Treasurer. All our officers were deliberately chosen from different parts of the country. Our vice-president was from New York and we had members of our Executive Board from Cleveland, Detroit, California, and Texas.

I had an office in Washington. First we were at U Street at 9th in the Dixon Building, then we moved across the street from McGuire's Funeral Parlor on 9th Street, to Mrs. Smith's place. She had a nice first floor right on the street. Then one of the Brotherhood men bought a house on 817 Q

Street and rented it to us, so there was room enough for the Brotherhood office, for my office, and also recreation space. The New York headquarters supplied me with all the necessary office supplies and I was able to open my office almost immediately. Sister Wilson had her office in Chicago. The other international women officers did not have too much work and performed in their homes.

It was my business to collect dues, send out all supplies, and keep a record of all business. The supplies were ordered. I would send to New York and they would order them from a union printer and send them to me. I had to examine them and let the sender know whether there were any discrepancies in the money and the like. I had to keep a record of every member in the entire set-up. I had a fine secretary, Mrs. Virginia Harris, a young lady who became almost like a daughter to me. From time to time, Cardozo High School sent two or three students to help. They got credit in school for the work they did for me. I also paid them, although not too much, as I was not getting very much myself. When these young people graduated, I often wrote letters of recommendation for them and they got various positions because of that.

Chapter XV--Civic Work

From the time I married Berthea, I was active in civic work. In the late 20s, I was visited by two young women from the neighborhood who asked me if I would be interested in helping them organize a club for the purpose of doing something constructive, rather than for mere pleasure. There were many clubs in the neighborhood, but they were mainly card clubs. But these women were not interested in bridge and other parlor games. They wanted to do something constructive and invited me to join them. I was interested in the proposed project and joined them. Soon other women, many of them school-teachers, joined. We called ourselves the Northeast Women's Club. I was its president for 15 years. We met in our homes, paid a nominal monthly fee, had teas, served dinners in the neighborhood and arranged it so that we could serve in teachers in the neighborhood schools at lunch time. We were very successful in raising the needed funds

Almost immediately, our attention was directed to children of the area who did not have adequate clothing or shoes. As far as possible, the club supplied the necessary clothing and then informed the parents where to go for shoes, since the District Government furnished shoes to school children from a special fund for needy students. We supplied food and paid rent for indigent families to tide them over rough spots; we gave car fare [i.e. money to ride the streetcars]

to students who lived too far away to walk to school, and when we learned that the safety patrol boys needed raincoats and caps, we furnished the money to buy them. During this period, citizens brought to our attention the need for more lights on many dark streets and alleys, and traffic signals at dangerous intersections. In many instances, our requests were granted.

Thus, we found ourselves knee-deep in social service work. Most of the contacts to the District officials were made by me. One of my duties and pleasures was helping to prepare children for summer camp. The Board of Charities was a District organization that looked after the poor and needy, supplying food, clothing, and other necessities. In the summer, selected needy children were sent to camp at Blue Plains for two weeks. Mothers with babies, needing rest, went also. The babies were placed in a separate area and cared for by a person trained to take over their care, bathing, dressing, and feeding them, and supervising their sleeping periods. Before leaving for camp, all were examined by the doctor stationed there for that purpose. I was there to assist the children when being examined by the doctor, to see that their credentials were correct. Then I would take as many as my green Studebaker would hold to the camp in Blue Plains, DC, which was then a very rural area. The next Sunday afternoon I would visit the camp to see that all was well.

It was indeed heart-warming to see these mothers relieved of the many tasks of the home and the concern for their children's safety in the big city, sitting in rocking chairs in the cool shade of spreading trees, truly relaxed for at least two weeks. This was compensation enough to me for all my efforts towards helping them to get to camp.

One parent here in my neighborhood wanted her little girl in camp and asked me to help her. I did and when her daughter returned, her mother was so grateful, for not only did the child have a pleasant outing, but she learned so much while there that prepared her to help in her own home.

One of our deepest concerns for our area was the lack of school facilities for colored children. The area covered by the Northeast Women's Club was bounded by Florida Avenue on the north, 15th Street on the east, H Street on the south, and the railroad tracks on the west. When I first became involved, there were an equal number of white and colored children in the school area, but, as the years went by, the number of white children declined, while the number of colored children increased dramatically. There was no school in this area for the colored children and two for the white, Hayes and Blair. Each had a capacity for 320, yet, in

1930 Hayes had only 155 and Blair 182. The colored children had to go to Logan School at 3rd and G Streets, N.E., Lovejoy, at 12th and D, N.E., or Slater, Langston, Cook, or Bundy. All were beyond our school area and too far for small children to walk. Many parents had to accompany them to and from school, which was a hardship to the parents and an expense, as most parents had to use public transportation.

Now, the First Assistant Superintendent of the schools was Garnet Wilkinson, who had partial charge of the colored schools. Mr. Wilkinson graduated from the old M Street High School the year I entered that school. While we had never formally met each other, I knew that he had seen me many times, for I was one of the three students who played a march on the piano for the student body when it came into the assembly hall each morning for devotions. I went to see him relative to our need for schools. We had a pleasant conversation, and Mr. Wilkinson reminisced how he walked from his home in Anacostia every morning to high school and back in the evening—which was quite a walk. However, he said that for the time being he was unable to provide more schools. It was only many years later that we were granted our wish.

Our Northeast Women's Club noted that Dunbar and Armstrong High School students received a gift at their graduation exercises and we decided to remember the Margaret Murray Washington Vocational School graduates in a similar way. Our gift of money was small, but it was appreciated by the principal, Miss Randolph[74], and the students who were the recipients. This we continued over a period of many years. Many of the school teachers who were active members of this club were given credit by the school system for their work with us and many received promotions for such work.

It was brought to my attention that we were performing the services of a civic association without be recognized as such. Some years before this, there had been a civic association in this area, the Public Interest Civic Association, but it had not functioned for some time. Women had been barred from membership. I understood that it was really a "men's club" at best, not interested sufficiently with the problems of the neighborhood.

In 1942 Dr. Edward Harris,[75] president of the Federation of Civic Associations, heard of our activities and asked me if I would revitalize the Public Interest Civic Association. I discussed it with some members of the community, and they were happy at the thought. Dr. Harris

---

[74] Leona C. Randolph, principal of the school from 1919 to 1943.

[75] Edward F. Harris was a black pharmacist

advised me to invite as many of the members of the defunct organization as I could contact, also invite the members of the Northeast Women's Club and all other citizens who might be interested in meeting for the purpose of revitalizing and reorganizing the Public Interest Civic Association. We met in Calvary Episcopal Church. There was an impressive number of citizens present, both men and women. Almost everybody in the Northeast Women's Club was there. Dr. Harris presided over the election of officers. I was unanimously elected president, Dr. Jesse Keen, a former member, first vice president, Mr. James Pride, recording secretary, Mr. George D. Brown, corresponding secretary, and Mr. Charles Williams, a member of the original association, treasurer. After I was elected, I asked Dr. Harris to address the meeting. He came, gave us a boosting talk and we were on our way. Each area association was required to send the president and four other delegates to the Federation, and this was the beginning of my activities with that group.

The Public Interest Civic Association joined the Federation of Civic Associations. Each of our five delegates was placed on a committee. Dr. Harris, the president, assigned me to the chairmanship of the Social Service and Welfare Committee. We had the responsibility for providing care to the aged, the feeble-minded, dependent and delinquent children, and the homeless.

Since my committee could not cover all of the services in detail, we gave special attention to the National Training School for Colored Girls, which provided vocational education, and the Industrial Home for Colored Boys, whose function was to provide institutional care for boys who needed it, including protection, supervision, food, shelter, and medical care. Many a Sunday afternoon Dr. Harris and I and some of the committee members would visit the boys' School at their regular Sunday afternoon public exercises at which time the boys would sing and recite. We also attended similar exercises at the girls' school. I remember that we gave the boys a ping-pong table and each girl toothpaste and a brush, toilet soap, and face-powder. Each school was supplied with footballs (for the boys), basketballs, and other balls of all shapes and sizes.

I became so interested in the girls' school that I was considered as being a part of it. One day I met one of the officials of the Federation, who asked me, "How are your girls getting along?" Frankly, I was puzzled. I told him that I had two boys, but no girls. Noting my confusion, he said, "I mean your girls at the Training School." Well, I considered this a signal compliment, for I was happy to be identified with this group of girls and to serve in this area where the need was so pressing.

When I visited the school for the feeble-minded, I was deeply impressed with the unfortunate children therein. No matter how extensive their affliction, I was sensitive to their desire for love and understanding, for so many of them—and these were white children—would meet me with outstretched arms, inviting me to take them into mine. Not only at this particular school, but at other institutions, it was only necessary to look into the eyes of these disturbed children to see the conflict in their souls.

At Junior Village, there were children who were orphans, others who had been abandoned, many of whom from birth had known no other home but that institution. During the Christmas season we encouraged people to invite one or two of these children to spend a few days, or at least Christmas day, at their home. Some people enjoyed having two or more of these children with them for as long as two weeks.

I visited an institution for homeless boys whose ages were from six to 15 years. I do not remember the exact location of the school, but it was in New York State and not far from Brooklyn. There were so many of these unfortunate children. While I was reviewing the building with the superintendent, there came meal time, and those boys filed into the dining room and there commenced the long ceremony of prayers and songs before being allowed to be seated to eat the meager meal served on tin plates, in tin cups with tin forks and spoons. I stood there and cried. I could not hold the tears back. These boys had no homes, no parents to give them the tender care so necessary during that period of their development. However, this institution as well as others of its kind should be commended as pioneers of the present institutions which today are built more consistent to the housing requirements of the inmates with better preparation and serving of food, better prepared teachers, better school facilities, and better recreation.

In quiet moments I still think of this group of boys and how they made my heart cry out in sympathy for them. I know that many of them have passed on, and those who yet live could be grandfathers, but as they were fed and shielded from the heat of summer and the cold of winter, though inadequately, I hope that they themselves in the interim have served others in whatever capacity they were able, no matter how small or how great.

There is a verse of Scripture that has intrigued me for a number of years. It is: "Whoever will save his life shall lose it; but whosoever will lose his life for my sake, the same shall save it." A paradox, you say? Truly, for it is hard to understand; nevertheless it is true, for only those who actually lose themselves serving others can understand this seeming contradiction. Only those who serve selflessly can attain that plateau of saving their own life.

When the United States entered World War II in late 1941 I enrolled in the United States Civil Defense Corps and in 1942 I was certified as a Food and Housing Warden, entitled to wear the official emblem and insignia appropriate to the office. I called together everybody I could, white and colored, to a meeting at Mount Olive Baptist Church on 6th Street, between L and M Streets, N.E. to inform them what each could do to help the war effort. We formed Red Cross classes. Trained personnel were sent to teach us first aid and how to be food wardens. Transportation units were formed for those who had cars. We learned all the signals pertaining to the air raids and shelters. We were on guard at all times. Everyone who took the training received a certificate for the course. I received three certificates.

During the years that I was active in the Brotherhood, in the Northeast Women's Club, and in the Federation, I was also involved in the NAACP. My association with the National Association for the Advancement of Colored People began in the 1920s. I became active in the Washington local, working closely with Attorney Eugene Davidson, Sr., who was the head of the chapter at that time. It was through him that I made the acquaintance of W.E.B.

DuBois and Walter White, two of the guiding lights of that organization. Mr. White was a small, prim man whose skin coloring was white. He used his skin coloring, however, to benefit his people, for, in order to get information to benefit the NAACP, he would pass for white and talk to white people, especially in the South, to learn of various attitudes and activities that would be of benefit to the NAACP. Dr. DuBois was a fine gentleman, very impressive and highly educated. He was dynamic as a speaker and was instrumental in getting some colored people to vote Democratic. In those days, black people were Republican, but many, when asked the reason for their preference, would reply, "'Cause Lincoln was Republican and Lincoln freed our people." By now, however, the Republican Party had come to take the black vote for granted. They no longer cared, as a rule, whether Negroes were treaty fairly or not. They were making no major effort to improve conditions. I remember hearing a particular speech by DuBois, in which he urged the necessity of at least dividing the vote. "I know," he said, "that Lincoln, you say, freed the slaves, but just remember, Lincoln is dead and you are not voting for Lincoln."

Chapter XVI—Henry

Willard Corrothers was married only a few months when he was drafted into the Army in 1917. Immediately on his return from the war, he and his wife separated and he went west to live. I was to hear from him again only once, when he wrote Henry that he had read several articles in newspapers of the success of a "Hank" Corrothers as a winning football coach. He wrote, "Are you my long-lost brother?", then added, "I guess it was I and not you who was lost." He expressed surprise that Henry chose the field of Physical Education because he had always envisioned him as a doctor. He noted that he liked the southern California climate, that he was an electrician and the inference was that he was doing well. When Henry received the letter, he sent it to me to answer, as it was October, one of the busiest months for a football coach. Inasmuch as Willard's birthday was near—November 2, I sent him a birthday card and a note, using the address indicated on the letter. The card was returned, stamped "Addressee Unknown." I later learned that Willard was passing as a white man. Over the years I have been urged to use well-known methods of finding lost relatives, but refrained from this because, if Willard is passing for white, there may be a wife and children, and my fears is an irreparable disruption of his family if I pursued this course. Even to this day I wonder and worry about the man-child I reared as my own. He is over 80 years old now. Perhaps it is too much to hope that Willard is still alive—yet I'm alive at 97.[76]

My natural son, Henry, remained close to me. He loved all kinds of sports before his high school days. His father considered football too rough a game for youngsters to play. But at West Chester, Pennsylvania, where we lived, the local "home boys" formed a team as did the boys at Cheyney, which was not far away. Once, when they met in a contest, a boy from the West Chester team was injured as was a member of the Cheyney team. We learned of the incident when phone calls were exchanged regarding the extent of their injuries. At dinner that night we were able to pull out of Willard that he was playing that he was playing against the Cheyney team, and the boy who was injured was a friend and member of his home team. Willard told us, "So the next time the Cheyney boy came through the line, I knocked him out cold." Henry thereupon commented jokingly, " Willard, didn't you know that was a football game, not a boxing match?" We had a good laugh at

---

[76] Willard was indeed alive at the time that Mrs. Tucker wrote about him, but died September 26, 1981, at the age of nearly 87, a few weeks before his stepmother's hundredth birthday, without contact being re-established.

Henry's statement. You see, their father taught them how to box, but forbade them to play football.

After their father died and Willard went into the Army, Henry and I moved back to Washington, as I recounted earlier, and Henry entered the Dunbar High School. I did not know that he was in training for the football team until one night when he did not come home. When, to my relief, Henry arrived the next morning, he had to explain that he had played in a game in Manassas, Virginia, and the team, coaches, and officials had missed the train and had to spend the night there. Henry was relieved and pleased when I took the episode in stride.

When I was very ill in Freedman's Hospital that winter, Henry, when visiting me one day, told me that he had quit school and had a government job. After two years he saw no prospects of promotions, although he had the ability to train white workers who *did* obtain promotions. He then decided to return to school. After his graduation, I suggested that he go to Howard University here in Washington. Henry demurred, saying that he knew too many Howard students, "And, besides, Howard students do not have too much success if they live here." What he meant was that he was seeking a school with a less distracting environment. I was quite worried when Henry announced his desire to go to Virginia Union University in Richmond, Virginia. I was still perplexed when I met on the street my high school English teacher, Dr. Riggs. I told her that my son did not want to go to Howard University, but to Virginia Union in Richmond. Dr. Riggs' words were, "You should let him go. The influences there are very good." I thanked her and told her how relieved I was. He went to that school and really found himself.

While at Virginia Union, Henry and many of the students went to Atlantic City to work during the summer season. Henry had never been to a summer resort before, so everything was new to him. The first summer he worked for a woman who owned a boarding house with many rooms. Henry wrote to me, "Mom, I thank you for teaching me how to sweep, dust, mop, wash windows, and such, for I have plenty of that to do." He told me that when the house was full, the proprietress became almost a nervous wreck and "I find myself taking over some of her duties," until her composure was restored.

Henry worked at the boarding house for two seasons, but when her letter came the third season, he had decided to seek a better position. That summer he wrote to me, "I have taken a position at Fraylinger's on the boardwalk as a syrup mixer and a soda dispenser, and Mom, I don't know a thing about it." I went down in prayer for him. The next week he wrote, "I have done so well that I have employed Pope Gregory [a friend], as my assistant.."

His job the next year was for a French confectioner on the boardwalk, where all kinds of French ices, creams, sodas, and pastries with French names were served. There was a table that stretched the length of the room upon which were numerous glass and silver dishes, containing all sorts of fruits, nuts, syrups, and toppings. I saw the establishment myself, for Henry had planned a trip for me while he was there. When patrons came into the place, they would look at the list of items, and indicate what they wanted (usually not knowing what they were ordering, as the menu was in French). Henry did not know what they were ordering, either! He said he would put down the basic item, usually ice cream, in the appropriate dish and then go down the length of the table, putting a little of this and a little of that on, making it attractive to look at, and then serve it. "If the same persons were to come in again and indicate the same item," he said, "they certainly would not get exactly the same combination!"

There were three football players at Virginia Union University who were instrumental in winning games for the school. The team won the championship in their particular league three of the four years those students were there. These three were given the title "The Great." So it was Pope

Gregory "the Great", James Jones "The Great", and Hank Corrothers "The Great." James Jones became an outstanding dentist and Gregory became a mortician of note. Henry was captain three of the fur years that he was at Union and after every game he proudly wired me the score.

When Henry finished Union, he told me of an offer he had received. "Mom," he told me, "I can be an assistant coach now."

"*Assistant* coach?" I exclaimed. "I don't want you to be an assistant *anything*! If you go into something, be prepared to go into it the whole way. If you want to be a coach, be a fully prepared coach."

So Henry sent his application to Springfield College in Springfield, Massachusetts. At that time, the college required a letter from a minister, a doctor, and a layman, so we had them write to Dr. Grimke, for the letter from the minister. The next Sunday, Dr. Grimke, during the service, asked me to come to the rostrum at the close of the service. In his quiet, cold manner, he told me that he had received a letter from Springfield College, that he did not know my son, and therefore, could not recommend him. Well, Henry had been away much of the time we had lived in Washington, going to school, then off to work, but all we wanted was a simple letter, stating that he was a member of the church. I thanked Dr. Grimke and told him that it was all right, but I was deeply hurt, for Henry *was* a member. So, I wrote to Dr. Lee, Poet's good friend, explaining the situation. "Mrs. Tucker, have no further concern," he wrote back. "*I know Henry Corrothers.*" So, Dr. Lee wrote to Springfield College and Henry, my son, had no difficulty matriculating there.

One midnight, late in September, Henry called me from Atlantic City, saying that he had finished his work there, that he had all his clothes and they were packed for traveling, that he had sufficient money for everything but books. "What shall I do, go on to Springfield or back to Union?" (If he had gone back to Virginia Union, it would have been as assistant coach.). Deep down within me, while still holding the receiver, I prayed, "God, help me to decide." After a moment, I felt led to answer, "Go to Springfield." I had to make the decision *then*, for every hour Henry remained in Atlantic City meant a drain on his funds. When Berthea came home two days later, he took me to task for not consulting him first. But I was unable to impress him that the decision could not wait.I have never regretted that decision. I knew that Henry would do all he could to help himself, even in areas of work unfamiliar to him, as proven by his efforts in Atlantic City. So I gave him moral and financial support at all times.

Joseph Smith, Berthea's nephew, was one of four brothers, reared by their older sister in Petersburg, Virginia, after their parents died. He was now living in Springfield, Massachusetts. Henry was invited to live with him while he was at Springfield College. A few months later, Joe married Ethel Robinson and Henry was his best man at the wedding. Joe and Ethel enjoyed having Henry with them during those years. Joe did extra work during the day for wealthy householders who trusted no one else to handle their valuable glassware, dishes, silverware, and fine furnishings, but his main job was cleaning offices at night for a large insurance company. Joe told me that many times Henry would go downtown at night and help him do his work. Ethel had several brothers and sisters who became very close to Henry and me, and called me "Aunt Rosina." Henry, who was exceptionally outgoing, soon made friends not only of the Smith family, but, it seemed, practically everyone in Springfield. They called him "Hank", but I never called him that.

From childhood I counseled my sons to be kind and considerate of everyone, regardless of their status. Thus, when Henry entered Springfield College, his friendly and unassuming personality resulted in his being in constant demand as a referee for informal games in the city and surrounding communities. Discussing such engagements with me he would say, "Mother, I thank you," for it meant much needed money for a student still in school.

Henry applied for a job on a playground in Washington, DC for the summer after his first year at Springfield College. This was in line with his future work. He said that he was not sure that he would get it, because another student from another college had applied also, and since the other student's father was "in the system", Henry was sure that he would lose out. I turned to my son and said, "Do you really want the job?"

He said, "Yes, I do."

I said to him, "System or not system, you'll get it." He looked at me in a puzzled manner, and I added, "God is greater than any 'system' in the world.!"

When Henry left the room, I went down in prayer. Henry was a member of the Omega Fraternity, and that year he was made "Summer Basileus."[77] As was his want, he worked assiduously, building the fraternity in numbers and interest. One day he met Dr. Herbert Marshall, Sr., a distinguished Georgetown physician, who complimented him on the work that he was performing for the fraternity. Henry thanked him and, in his practical manner, said, "But if I cannot get work here, I will have to go when I *can* get

---

[77] Whoever typed this section of the autobiography wrote "Bacillus." I rather think a fraternity would more likely to honor someone by calling him a king ("basileus") than a *bacterium!*

work. I have applied for work on the playgrounds, but I have gotten no response."

Dr. Marshall said, "I know the director and I will talk to her and you'll get the job."

Henry got the job. My prayers were answered. I would not have one believe that the job was gotten by "pull" or "influence" for Henry, as he had proven himself qualified, and, God, in answer to my prayer, arranged it that these two men (i.e. Henry and Dr. Marshall), were drawn together at the right time. It should be added that the young man whose father was "in the system" got a job on a playground also, so neither one was the loser.

In 1927 Henry, who had earned his B.A. degree from Virginia Union University, received a Bachelor's degree in Physical Education from Springfield College, having completed the four year course in two years. Much pressure was placed on him to accept positions at several colleges. Not only was he pressured by college officials, but also by alumni of various colleges, some of whom lived in Washington, DC and visited me, urging me to influence him to accept their college's proffers. However, the decision was my son's to make, not mine. Harry Graves, the director of Physical Education at Wilberforce University in Ohio challenged Henry, "Hank, come, let's put Wilberforce on he map," and after much thought, Henry decided to go there.

And the two of them did put Wilberforce U on the map. Henry's position at Wilberforce was that of Instructor of College Physical Education, and he was the coach of the football, track, and basketball teams. Later, he introduced boxing, and conducted Golden Gloves Tournaments for a Dayton, Ohio newspaper and developed a champion boxer. In 1935 and 1936 the football team won the Midwest Conference title. Henry also worked as a sports broadcaster.

Although Henry's work schedule at Wilberforce was heavy and exacting, he drove back and forth to Ohio State University at Columbus and obtained his MA degree in 1930. He received a certificate for special summer courses under Knute Rockne at Notre Dame University and for special courses under Pop Warner at Springfield University (in Ohio), and was writing his thesis for his Ph.D in education at the time of his death, some years later.

During those years I did a great deal of traveling in connection with my Union work, and wherever I went, it seemed as if everybody I met knew "Hank" Corrothers. So I made it a point to test people now and then to see if they knew him.

One Sunday morning I saw three big husky men sitting toward the rear of my church. Going to speak to them after the service, I inquired, "Do you play football?" They replied in the affirmative. "Where do you go to school?"

They said, "Johnson C. Smith."

"Do you know Hank Corrothers?"

"Oh, yes, Ma'am! He's the best football coach in the country!" And they rattled off his record.

Once I was on a train en route to Cleveland, Ohio, and talked to a man who said that he was in motion pictures and speared sharks for the movies. I asked, "Do you happen to know Hank Corrothers?"

"Oh, yes! He's the greatest athletic coach in the United States!" he said.

In my office I was introduced to a coach of our Normal School. When he learned that I was Hank Corrothers' mother, he kissed my hand and said, "He has helped me to be what I am today."

Once I asked a soldier in New York City if he had gone to college, and he said he had, before going to war. I then asked him if he knew Hank Corrothers. He embraced me, saying, "He has helped young men all over the country! Many of them are now among the finest coaches around."

Whenever Henry took me in his car, no matter how large or how small the city, everyone seemed to know him and was anxious to speak to him and he was proud to say, "Meet my mother."

Yet with all the attention paid him, there was never a trace of hauteur in his speech or action or bearing. My older son, Willard, would talk back to me at times, but he would not hesitate to fight anyone to the bitter end who offended me. Henry would fight also, but his understanding of and love for me was so deep that with one look he could tell my state of mind, especially if I was worried, and he knew intuitively how to comfort me

Chapter XVII–Family Matters

Berthea did not know half the things I was involved in, and, accordingly, I made it a rule to be a home whenever he was and to work out my other activities for such a time as he was on his runs. As time went on, Bert became quite difficult. I got little sympathy and encouragement from him. It was especially hurtful when I wanted to speak to him of my faith in Christ, that he continually dismissed with, "There you go with your crazy talk!" He bought an automobile but never could learn to drive, and was frustrated and resentful when I did. There were several intervals over the years when, to preserve peace of mind, I had to take extended "vacations" from my husband and yet remain in the city. During one period in the 20s, I lived apart from him for three years until a friend persuaded me to go back. "Don't let him keep you away from your home. That house belongs to you, too, so go back and enjoy it."

One may wonder why we did not get a divorce. We did love each other, even though at times we had grave trouble getting along. Moreover, I felt that my marriage to Berthea—and still feel—was meant to be. I believe that God has a plan for all of us and carries out His will in everything. My often tempestuous second marriage was part of His plan. St. Paul writes, "We glory in tribulations also, know that tribulation worketh patience; and patience, experience, and experience, hope." (Rom 5:3) Through overcoming the many obstacles in my marriage, through my faith in Christ, I have been able to help many others in similar predicaments. One must also remember that if I had not married Berthea, I would have never become involved with the Brotherhood, where God has permitted me, as I believe, to do a little good. So God can make every good every situation, and such he did with a marriage that many would have found unsatisfactory.

Over the years, I maintained close relation with my mother, brothers, and sisters. After her divorce from Marion Clinkscales, , who was a successful lawyer with a lot of business in the still-rural areas around Washington, Marietta married a man named Ike Alexander,[78] whom the rest of the family thought an unfortunate choice. Our worst expectations were realized, the marriage broke up after a short time, and poor Marietta fell on very hard times. She continued to give music lessons and serve as organist.

I was closest to my younger sister Nettie, who married George Brown. Nettie was one of the sweetest

---

[78] The census of 1920 shows Jeremiah M. Alexander, age 48, an upholsterer, born in North Carolina, living at 1232 Linden Street, N.E., with his wife Marietta, a teacher, and his mother-in-law, Henrietta Harvey, a servant in a "private family."

people I have ever known. Her husband was custodian of an apartment building in Northeast and Nettie was a homemaker. That is what she considered to be her calling. She was a wonderful cook, and "I can fix up anything," was her boast. Whenever I was ill, she would always come over, and from whatever leftovers she found in the refrigerator, she was able to make a wonderful meal. In January, 1922, we had more than two feet of snow. This was the storm in which the Knickerbocker Theater at 18th and Columbia Road, N.W., collapsed, killed 100 people. The snow virtually paralyzed traffic, but Nettie, knowing that I was sick in bed, left her house anyway. No trolleys were running, nor could she find any cabs to hail. However, seeing a truck, she called to its driver, "My sister is sick. Can you let me ride along to see if she is all right?" The driver consented and Nettie got here, snow and all. When Henry was in college, Nettie would send boxes of food to him and his friends. She was the most generous person, I think, that God ever created, and she was a devoted Christian, too.

 I was close to my brother Harry. While I was living out of town, married to Poet, Harry went to school in Lynn, Massachusetts. Upon his return, he married and had two children, Ethel and Hugh[79]. Due to difficulties between Harry and his wife Pearl, the children were not permitted to visit members of our family. Mom was especially heart-broken that of her three grandchildren, two she saw little of. For of her five children who lived to maturity, Harry and I were the only ones to whom God granted offspring. And neither of us was particularly prolific. At any rate, finally Harry and Pearl separated. Late in 1928, Nettie found Harry living, alone and sick, in a rented room and asked if I would take him in. He had fallen into ill health because of his wife's nagging. I conferred with Berthea, and he consented. So, Harry came to live with us, but after a short time it became evident to both of us that my brother was a very sick man, and the hospital was the place for him. Removed to a hospital, Harry died after a week or two, in January, 1929. He was only 42.

Harry's death was the beginning of a rapid diminution in my family circle. Within a decade, God saw fit to take from me most of my immediate family. One day in October, 1930 I got a phone call from my brother-in-law, George Brown. "Is Nettie there?" he asked. I told him she was not. He phoned Ben and asked him the same question,

---

[79] The 1920 census shows Harry A. Harvey, 33, an office clerk, living at 1450 Florida Avenue, N.W.,, with his wife, Pearl C., age 34, also an office clerk, and their two children, Ethel, 10, and Hugh W. 8.

but my brother had to respond in the negative, too. Worried, Ben began to comb the newspapers and found an article about an unidentified woman being picked up off the street just a few blocks from where George and Nettie owned their home. He went to the morgue and identified the body as Nettie's. She was in the habit of going to a store every day for ice cream, and it was on this routine errand that day that she suffered a heart attack and fell dead, a short distance from her home.

That left just Ben, Marietta, Mom, and myself of the original family circle. Ben was a fine man. Although he was not a church man, one could always depend on him for everything. One day in 1934 he called me on the phone. "Rose," he said, "I have had some medical exams and the doctors have diagnosed cancer of the throat. Now I know I cannot live for very long. I want you to take Mom into your home." I did this and Ben entered the Mount Alto [Veterans Administration] Hospital on Wisconsin Avenue, where he stayed for nearly a year. One day Marietta called. She claimed to be psychic and maintained, "I've had my sign. You get Mom and go over and see Ben." So I got my mother, who was by then 82^{80} and suffering from arthritis, dressed her and put her in the car, and off we went. It was

---

[80] If the census of 1870 is correct, Henrietta Harvey was then about 90.

not until we were on our way that I asked her, "Mom, who you think we're going to see?"

"I don't know, Rose."

"We are going to see Ben."

Her face lighted up and she seemed so happy. When we got there, Ben seemed alert and cheerful and did not seem to be suffering or in pain. All of us were encouraged by the visit and Mom never stopped expressing her delight on the way back and for the rest of the evening as to how well Ben seemed and that how he might recover after all. Early the next morning, the phone rang. Ben was dead. Shortly after that, his wife Bessie went to pieces and soon afterwards died.

Mom had now lost all but two of her nine children. She never went to pieces. She took everything very calmly. I often wonder how she felt, during the watches of the night, about losing seven of her nine children, about losing practically everybody. But there was something about the women of her generation that endured such things. It was Mom's great faith in Christ and in the Resurrection that sustained her and enable her to undergo this chastening without bitterness and without despair. Today, many women are resentful when they lose a child and embittered when their husband dies. I remember seeing recently a woman on television who had written a book about her bereavement.

She said she was at first angry at her husband for dying. This dumbfounded me. Such sentiments are alien to me. God is in charge of our span of life. Mom knew this and she also knew that for those whose faith is in Jesus Christ, death is not the end, but the beginning. But not too many people believe this way anymore. Even then, there were some people who did not. In contrast to Mom, I had a friend my own age at Fifteenth Street Church.[81]

When her oldest daughter[82] died under tragic circumstances, neither she nor her younger daughter were ever seen in church after that[83]. Along with my good friend, Mrs. Elizabeth Hall, I worried about this family and ultimately discovered that their absence was due to the fact that they had grown resentful towards God for taking the young woman away. For years the family set the lost daughter's picture in a prominent place in their home and set flowers before it and smothered it with kisses. But Mom did not grieve as one who had no hope.

---

[81] Blanche Kemp Ruffin (1884-1958)

[82] Viola Robinson Burgess (1899-1928)

[83] Blanche Ruffin (my grrandmother), did eventually return to church. Her daughter Elinor, however, never did, and to the end of her life expressed the sentiment, "How could God let Sissie die?"

Eventually came Mom's turn to rest. In her later years, although her mind was very alert, Mom suffered with arthritis. But, despite my other activities, I took care of her in my home, as I had done ever since Ben's hospitalization. Suddenly, one day in the summer of 1938, Marietta insisted that I let Mom live with her. At first I was reluctant. I was confused. When Ben had become ill, Marietta had said that she could not take Mom. Now she was insistent that Mom come with her. I went to Dr. Taylor, my pastor, as I did on many different occasions, to consult him about personal matters. I told him the situation and he said, "Now, Mrs. Tucker, let her go. Let your sister have her. There is nothing worse than what can happen with family quarrels. Rather than have anything of that sort, I think you had better let your mother go." So, Mom went to live with Marietta in an apartment in a large house in the Brookland section of Washington, where the owner, Mr. Lucas, an old family friend, had amassed an impressive collection of statuary and beautiful flowers in the back yard. Mom had not been with my sister two weeks before she died.

I had been struck by an automobile and slightly injured but had not told Mom. A few days after I took her to my sister's, I went to Asheville, North Carolina, for a rest with my dear friends, Mr. and Mrs. Benjamin F. McLaurin. While there, I got word that Mom was in a coma. By the time I reached Washington that next evening, August 14, she was gone. Mom was 85.[84] Through all this I felt that God had helped me. He had enabled me to take care of her. Marietta commented that she wondered how I had been able to care for her, as Mom was an extraordinarily heaven woman, and she found it difficult to lift her and attend to her needs. But, perhaps it was because God enabled me that I never found Mom hard to lift or move. I think the fact that I had to relinquish Mom's care to my sister was God's way of sparing me the anguish of seeing her die. I am very grateful that in the course of my long life, God has spared me the sight of actually witnessing the death of most of my loved ones. Their last sufferings might have affected me adversely.

---

[84] More likely 93.

Chapter XVIII-The March on Washington

It was in 1941, with war clouds brewing over our side of the Atlantic that Brother Randolph first conceived of a March on Washington. In the years since the Brotherhood was recognized by the Pullman Company, it had become a member of the American Federation of Labor, and had grown to be quite powerful. It had obtained jobs in various areas never before held by black men, most notably as conductors on the New York subway trains.

The March on Washington was conceived not only in behalf of railroad workers, but in behalf of all black people. The Washington local and ladies auxiliary began at once to organize for the event by renting the second floor of a large restaurant on the corner of 7th and S Streets, N.W. Setting up offices, the auxiliary decorated the rooms, equipped them with desks, typewriters, and other equipment for the officials and secretaries. The third floor was reserved to house marchers who should be unable to find other accommodations.

I had hoped that the march—and I told Mr. Randolph this—would be similar (in organization, though not in results) to the Bonus March which I witnessed nearly a decade earlier. The marchers, who were veterans from World War I, had built a regular city with streets on the

Anacostia Flats. They built barracks of tin cans and cardboard boxes. Henry was in town at the time and we both drove out to see this marvelous town they had built almost overnight. People came in droves to visit and they gave food and cigarettes and money to these veterans. They were a group fine, serious-minded men, both black and white. The march itself was an astounding thing. It was really impressive! There were the veterans, many dressed in their fatigues, marching up Pennsylvania Avenue. They said nothing, there was no music; the only sound was the thud of their shoes (some almost worn out) on the asphalt. The march was unsuccessful, however, and the veterans who wanted an increase in their pension[85] were driven away with some bloodshed. However, I told Mr. Randolph about the logistics of the march and he was deeply impressed. I knew that our march would be carried out in the same quiet manner. But it turned out that it was not necessary for us to march.

When he heard about the plans for the march, President Roosevelt was quite disturbed and sent Mrs. Roosevelt to New York. Along with the Mayor, Fiorello H. LaGuardia, Mrs. Roosevelt met with Mr. Randolph.

---

[85] They wanted an immediate cash payment redemption of their Service Certificates, which were not redeemable until 1945.

I had met Mrs. Eleanor Roosevelt at a meeting at Miner Teachers' College in Washington and had been impressed. It was a meeting to discuss Negro housing. The "Big Niggers" were all there, the men in their swallow-tailed suits and the women with their spangles and bangles. In contrast, Mrs. Roosevelt was wearing a plain long black dress with a simple necklace of pearls. She was such a contrast to the representatives of the Negro Elite. I came to know her as a splendid genteel woman.

I also knew Mayor LaGuardia well. He was an honorary member of the Brotherhood and I frequently met him at the many Brotherhood of Sleeping-Car Porters' meetings he attended in New York. He was short and somewhat pudgy, but quite pleasant and sincere. He would stand on the podium and say, "Now, I'm going to do so and so for the people of New York City." And he always did what he said he was going to do. The people were very fond of him. I can still see him at one of our meetings, resplendent in all his regalia, surrounded by his train of aides. At any rate, when Mrs. Roosevelt and Mayor LaGuardia met with Mr. Randolph, Mrs. Roosevelt said that the President was very preoccupied with the European war that American might at any time be forced into, and that he wished the march called off. Mr. Randolph replied, "Oh, no, we're not going to call it off."

Mrs. Roosevelt implored Randolph, but in vain. Mayor LaGuardia then told Mrs. Roosevelt, "No, Mrs. Roosevelt, if Phil says he's not going to call that march off, he isn't going to call it off." Mr. Randolph agreed, however, to a meeting with the President, at which time he was prevailed upon to call off the march, but only when President Roosevelt agreed to issue Executive Order 8802, which banned discrimination in industries holding government contracts. A Committee on Fair Employment Practices was set up, which eventually resulted in legislation to open many jobs to black people for the first time.

Twenty-two years later, in 1963, Mr. Randolph called upon all Americans around the country to join him in a demonstration to give Negroes their full civil rights. His call was heeded and on the designated day they came to Washington, D.C. The clergy was represented by all faiths—all branches of Baptists and Methodist; Presbyterians; Episcopalians; Catholics; Church of Christ and others. There were legislators, state and federal, organized labor of all branches, representatives from the NAACP, the Urban League, fraternal organizations, actors, dancers, singer. From the affluent areas of our country as well as from the slums they can, in high-powered cars and in tin lizzies. They came in chartered buses, ordinary buses and in chartered air flights. In fact, all strata of our society came here to meet at the Lincoln Memorial for Mr. Randolph's appeal to show the world that we are united in our quest and determination to claim our full civil rights. This was the largest gathering of Americans ever held in America. Mr. Randolph had invited many distinguished persons to speak and among them was Dr. Martin Luther King, Jr, a guest speaker. He had nothing to do with organizing The March. It was here that he deliver his speech "I Have a Dream." The public identified The March with Dr. King, whereas there never would have been such a demonstration if it had not been for Mr. Randolph and the Brotherhood of Sleeping-Car Porters and its Ladies' Auxiliary.

During the war I attended a labor banquet in New York, sponsored by the Brotherhood, in which Mrs. Roosevelt was the speaker. I was with her and others on the platform.

I almost failed to get there. Mr. Randolph was to mail my ticket and other particulars relative to my appearance there, but by the time it was necessary for me to get ready to leave, the envelope had not come. I called New York and was informed that the letter had been sent days ago. I did not know what to do. I left the house, praying to God to direct me. As I left my threshold, it occurred to me to go to 1128 7th Street *Northwest*. I was taking the wild risk that somehow the letter had arrived at the wrong address. I went to the Northwest address. It was a men's shop. I inquired of the clerk and he went upstairs and brought down a whole box of my mail, including the awaited letter, which had been delivered incorrectly. So I was able to attend the banquet.

When Mrs. Roosevelt appeared, the band played "Happy Days are Here Again." Mrs. Bethune was present. She came late and sat down beside Mrs. Roosevelt, who, in turn, was sitting just two chairs from me. I had the opportunity to observe Mrs. Roosevelt's every feature, every motion, every gesture, every emotion. She made much over Mrs. Bethune. "Oh, I'm so glad I'll be sitting next to my friend!" she said. There was in Mrs. Roosevelt a beauty of strength, a beauty of culture, a beauty of refinement that radiated from her features. On the surface, she was not attractive, although not nearly so unprepossessing in appearance as Mrs. Bethune, but intelligent and character shone through her homely features.

During the war and immediately afterward, when droves of black families were leaving their homes in the South for northern cities to better their living conditions, Union Station was where they had to transfer. One Sunday morning, before going to church to teach my Sunday school class, I decided to go over to the station to observe the vast number of travelers who were said to arrive Sunday mornings. The husbands and fathers were already working and had earned enough money to send for their families. It was in the concourse that I saw tragic scenes of black mothers struggling with four and five children, some mere babies, to make the change of trains. I found myself helping the mothers with their children, often taking one in my arm and another by the hand. This I repeated until all were aboard. I have often wondered how those children fared through the years. If living, some now could be grandfathers and grandmothers. I hope to this day that the parents found in their new locations the advantage they hoped for. It took much faith and courage for these families to leave the land of their birth for a land they knew not of. I am sure the change paid well for many of them in every area of their lives.

During the war years, when I was so feverishly working with the Brotherhood and the civic associations, many of my meetings with businessmen were held during the lunch hour, between twelve and two. I would go to my office on Q Street, work till a few minutes before twelve, then drive to the meeting and then return to work, working overtime, if necessary. It was important not to let my husband find out about my activities. The little he did learn made him violently furious. He would say, "Go on and work yourself to death!" My son took a different attitude. Henry was delighted in my work. "Why, you're just as versatile as you can be!" he would tell me.

Chapter XIX-Community Activist

Athletics had been de-emphasized at Wilberforce in the late 30s and Henry no longer had his position as coach. He remained as an instructor of physical education until 1943, when he left and went to Philadelphia. I never knew exactly why he left, but I know that he was not getting paid very much. I do not know exactly what he was doing in Philadelphia, but he said he was working on a project connected with the Government. I know that he supervised laborers and the men were very fond of him. They would come to him for help with their income tax. He was also working on his PhD at Columbia University. By that time he was divorced from his wife Reva. I do not know what went wrong. Henry did not talk about it.

In the spring of 1945, Henry fell sick.. At first he did not tell me, because he was afraid of worrying me. However, his great friend, Dr. Jones contacted me and told me that Henry was suffering from "pleuro-pneumonia." I immediately went up to Philadelphia to visit him in the hospital. He seemed fine to me. He seemed to be getting along all right. He talked with me and told me not to worry. I returned to Washington, relieved. However, a week later, Dr. Jones called me, saying that Henry had taken a turn for the worse and was very, very ill. Mr. Tucker had just returned from his run and when I told him that I was going to go away again, he was not pleased. I left that day, but I was too late. By the time I reached Philadelphia, Henry was dead.[86] He was 45.

It was a terrible tragedy. It was a terrible loss. I had Henry's body brought home to Washington. The funeral services were held at Fifteenth Street Presbyterian church. Mr. Tucker was not particularly helpful. Although he was fond of Henry, he refused to move a large chair out of the narrow hallway so that Henry's casket could be brought into the parlor. I had to have someone else do it. Perhaps he thought it belittling to himself to do things for me. But a neighbor observed that she had never seen a mother watch her son's casket brought into her home with as much calm as she saw in me. I suppose it was due to the lesson I had learned many years before from Mrs. Dunlap that I did not have to go through all the pain I went through when Poet died.. I am grateful to God for Henry and the 45 years He lent him to me and to others.

One Sunday morning, when I left home for Sunday School, I was rather disturbed. I taught my class and had gone upstairs for the morning service, which had not begun as yet. There was a woman sitting on the extreme end of the

---

[86] Henry Harvey Corrothers died April 28, 1945. According to his death certificate, his demise was caused by "bronchogenic carcinoma."

same pew. Suddenly, she quietly sort of slid next to me and said, "I love you." I was shocked and, not knowing what else to say, I said, "I love you, too." That "I love you" was just what I needed then, and God, through her, a stranger, satisfied my need.

One day three members of my fellowship and I went to a meeting in nearby Maryland. On our return, when we reached the business district, two of our members asked to be let out of the car to do some shopping. As we neared our destination, Mrs. Beatrice McMillan, the owner of the car, parked it and said, "Mrs. Tucker, I want to talk to you." She continued, "There are six women in our church who stop whatever they are doing at twelve o'clock every day and they pray together for you."

I said, "They pray for me?"

"Yes," she said. "They feel it's their duty when one of the members is distressed."

I wept aloud. To think that those women stopped whatever they were doing to pray for me! All the ice that had frozen within melted and left me by means of a flood of tears. This was truly joy that came to me through pain. This was the rainbow through the rain. I did not know until then my full capacity to love. I do not know who the other five women were, but I include them with all the women and men of the church within the circle of my arms of love.

I continued my work. In 1946, when a plebiscite was held relative to suffrage in the District, I had charge of two polling districts. The next year I was the only woman of my race on a committee of 24 that investigated the Community Chest of Greater Washington. I helped to write the minority report. The majority wanted to exclude such agencies as the YMCA and YWCA, both colored and white, as well as the Urban League. As a result of the minority report, the Chest was reorganized and these agencies were retained.

On June 10, 1946, I appeared before the Senate District Committee in the Capitol in behalf of Day Care Centers. I had come home from church very tired. I had told the folks at church, "I'm so tired, I'm going to bed." Around two or three, Mr. Woolsey Hall, the president of the Federation, called and said, "Mrs. Tucker, please cover a meeting for me. It's under your jurisdiction anyway." In other words, it was under the jurisdiction of the committee I chaired within the Federation.

I told him, "Mr. Hall, I can't do it."

"P-lease, Mrs. Tucker," he said. He really knew how to beg. "P-lease, Mrs. Tucker."

I asked him what it was all about.

"I'll send a lady there this afternoon," he promised.

I told him, "Don't you dare send her until about 5 o'clock."

She came at four and explained the details to me. I had to sit up all night and get things together so I could make a presentation which was acceptable.

The next day I spoke. After introducing myself as the President of the Public Interest Civic Association of Northeast Washington and the chairman of the Social Service and Welfare Committee of the Federation of Civic Associations, I told them that the Federation represented "the entire Negro citizenry of the District." I told them, "My organization is urging the passage of H.R. 5933. We are told that Washington has more working mothers than any other city of its size in the U.S. and that 500 mothers have used the facilities of the fourteen centers which have served 650 children." After explaining the conditions prevailing among many of the colored families in which the mother was the sole breadwinner, I concluded, "Is it not better to help these mothers build this kind of a home? Is it not better to help these mothers care for their children while they work and by so doing, help maintain a better home life? In many cases, the alternative would be public assistance, which is certainly not a morale-builder, or worse, more and larger penal institutions. I am sure that you, the committee, will agree that these mothers should be helped to maintain their home by the passage of H.R. 5933."

Present at the hearing were reporters from the newspapers, and when it came time for me to speak, they had gone out into the corridor. They must have been expecting Mr. Hall, the president. But when I got through, I was thunderously applauded by those who had crowded into the hearing room. The reporters then rushed into the room, all eager for me to give a synopsis of my speech. I said coldly, "I'll give you a copy," which they accepted.

Later, a committee from the Federation of Civic Associations had an interview with Representative Dawson[87], the colored representative from Chicago. There were about eight of us, each discussing the needs of the citizenry. I was the only woman. My topic covered schools, day care centers, and recreation. I told him, "In my area and in others there are no recreation facilities worthy of the name. When there are, they are not adequately staffed. There is a real need for more fully equipped centers over the entire city and provisions should be made to keep them open." All of us on this panel were presidents of the local civic associations. A newspaper reporting the hearing noted that when the other presidents spoke, Dawson seemed bored,

---

[87] William Levi Dawson (1886-1970), Representative from Illinois' First District from 1943 to 1970.

but when "this greying lady" talked about the schools, he took notice.

I also went to the offices of Senator Arthur Capper[88] of Kansas in my lobbying. Then over eighty, he was a fine-looking man with a shock of coal-black hair. He sat very straight. I told him how I remembered him years before when he rode a big, beautiful, well-groomed horse in Harding's inaugural parade. He was so pleased and flattered. "Any time you want any thing, come to see me," he said.

In 1953, it was decided to combine the Industrial Home for Colored Girls and the National Training School for Colored School for Colored Boys. There were some citizens who were disturbed when this decision was made, but a committee of interested citizens agreed that the move was necessary because of the poor physical condition of the buildings housing the girls and the fact that Congress would not appropriate funds for any improvements on that reservation. Then, too, the girls were under the influence of women teachers only, but, with the new arrangement, they would have some male instructors and thus, hopefully, would be able to father-figures. It was also felt that co-educational classes would be conducive to a more wholesome atmosphere and environment.

---

[88] Arthur Kapper (1865-1951), Senator from Kansas from 1919 to 1949.

The buildings into which the girls were to be moved were renovated and painted. I went to the reservation myself and inspected the two buildings to be used, to see that they were adequately equipped for occupancy by girls.

It was in the early 1950s that my committee, backed by the Federation of Civic Associations, was able to bring about the integration of the various institutions under the Board of Public Welfare. We did this by persistent agitation. I insisted that the conditions in the institutions be publicized and they were, in a series in the *Evening Star*. I had some strong words with officials regarding the situation in the Mount Olivet Receiving Home. Here boys and girls, having gotten into trouble, were detained until their cases were looked into by the courts. The facilities were racially segregated, and the Home was overcrowded. In order to make room for an increased number of white boys, the colored boys were moved from their quarters to the city jail! There was a meeting called about the overtaxed facility and I was the only colored person in attendance. Several prominent citizens were there, including Mrs. Agnes Myer, wife of the editor of the *Washington Post*. The police officer in charge spoke of the necessity of transferring the children to the jail because of the overcrowded conditions. Speaking with a mock earnestness and a faked concern, he was so mush-mouthed that I leapt to my feet and said, "You didn't put *your* boys in jail, did you? Then, why did you do this to *our* boys?" Everybody was startled by my outburst and became more so when I added, "I will take care of this situation immediately!" As a result of the meeting and my outburst, the practice was stopped, and soon the facilities were completely integrated.

There were people who wanted me on the school board and urged me to run. I was already very overworked, still being fully involved with the Brotherhood, and was very reluctant. But, because of constant and continual urging on the part of my friends and co-workers, I decided to think the matter over. I told Dr. Taylor about it. "Oh, Mrs. Tucker!" he said. "Why don't you let them put your name in? I will help you to get elected."

But I told him, "I have so much to do. I have a home to take care of, my husband is in and out, I have my Brotherhood work, too, and I just could not do it."

So, he agreed that I should decline the nomination.

During these years I was also nominated for a position on the Board of Recreation. I knew its director, Mrs. Alice Hunter, very well, and she would call on me many times with various problems. I was told that I had been nominated because my son had been distinguished in the field of Physical Education. I was even told that the Commissioners of Washington had been spoken to and that my procuring this job was virtually certain if I wanted it. Dr. Harris, the head of the Federation at the time, called on me at my home to ask my consent. Berthea was sitting over in the corner while Dr. Harris was talking. I did not say anything to him and he said nothing to me. But I worried all night long and could not sleep. The next morning, I asked Dr. Harris to withdraw my name. I also refused a position on the Board of Public Welfare. I just did not have time. In addition to my civic work and work with the Brotherhood, I was active in my church as trustee, Sunday School superintendent, as well as the teacher of the Young People's Class. I could not take anything more on.

Then, too, there was the problem of my husband. As I mentioned before, he seemed to resent anything I achieved. There was an incident at church where a man remarked to my husband, "Well, Mr. Tucker, you really have a wonderful wife. You must be proud of her." As a result of this, he sulked and stewed for days. At first I did not know the cause, and it was not until the following Sunday, when the man who had made the remark mentioned it me that I understood why Berthea had been so ill-natured the previous week.

Chapter XX-Travels for the Brotherhood

I was still active in the Brotherhood. President Randolph periodically asked me to represent him at many official functions. I would from time to time receive communications from him, like the following: "Dear Friend and Sister: I am enclosing a ticket to the Jefferson-Jackson Dinner, March 29 [1952] 7:30 PM. I will appreciate it if you will be my representative at the affair." The dinner was held at the National Guard Armory in Washington and was attended by President Truman and thousands of other people. I represented Mr. Randolph again five years later at a United Nations conference at the Mayflower Hotel in Washington.

I had a great deal to do as International Secretary-Treasurer of the Ladies' Auxiliary of the Brotherhood. That office, and not that of Vice-President, is next to that of President. I had to do a great deal of traveling, even into my seventies, as I took part in various programs and was asked to be the chief speaker at various programs put on by local auxiliaries in Boston, New York, Philadelphia, Denver, and other cities during these years. I was also called in to settle disputes.

I remember, in particular, a dispute within the New York branch. They requested that I be sent to them at once. They had to get permission from the International President,

Mrs. Wilson, who immediately insisted on coming there herself to mediate the dispute. She hurried in from Chicago to "get them told off." However, her manner was so overbearing that the New York ladies took offense. One of them snapped, "Who in the hell do you think you are? You're just another Pullman porter's wife, just the same as the rest of us!" Poor Mrs. Wilson failed to settle the dispute. "We told you to send Sister Tucker," one of the members said. "She knows how to handle us."

So, finally Sister Wilson consented and asked me to go to New York. I took the records from New York and also from Asheville, North Carolina. The latter was our youngest auxiliary and was doing splendid work. I wanted to compare the records to show how the more established branch in New York was comparing unfavorable with the newest in Asheville.

I do not know but that I talked to them worse than did Sister Wilson, but I think it was my manner that was different. When people know you and have confidence in you, you can say things to them that you could not otherwise. I said, "You know that I know you and what you can do. You ought to be ashamed of yourselves at not having done better. You have the New York office right here and you have no excuse for not doing better work." They did not ask "who the hell" I was and the dispute was settled. They gave me a two pound box of chocolates and on the spot took up eighteen dollars as a gift for me.

Over the years I did a lot of traveling in behalf of the Brotherhood. Brother Randolph often sent me because he knew I knew the work and would be able to make the contacts for him that were necessary.

It was my privilege in October, 1953 to travel with the Brotherhood on a special tour by train across country en route to the convention in Los Angeles. When it was finalized that Los Angeles would be our convention city that year, many porters' wives who had longed to visit California now had the opportunity to do so, and at greatly reduced rates. Ashley L. Totten, the International Secretary-Treasurer of the Brotherhood, had charge of such projects and, assisted by a committee of the international officials, urged the porters and their wives to invite relatives and friends to make reservation for this historic scenic tour.

The Brotherhood Special consisted of 18 Pullmans, two diners, and a recreation car. In the first window of each car was a neat black-on-white sign: "Brotherhood of Sleeping-Car Porters." We traveled to Chicago, and on October 1 we boarded the Brotherhood Special which carried us over the Chicago, Burlington, and Quincy Railroad, along the scenic route, stopping at Denver, Colorado Springs, Pike's Peak, the Royal Gorge, Pueblo, and the Continental

Divide. We stopped in Salt Lake City and saw the Mormon Tabernacle. Despite the somewhat racist attributes of the Mormon religion [at the time], we were treated cordially there.

As our special moved across the country, rural people along the route gazed as if entranced at the long line of Pullman cars, all filled with happy, dignified, and prosperous-looking black people. To all of us it was really a rewarding experience. Brother B.F. McLaurin, the supervisor of the Eastern Zone, had charge of the entertainment in the recreation car. The program consisted of speeches, singing, recitations, and interesting discussions, all of which were taped and played back to us for our pleasure and, in some instances, to our amusement. For months after the convention, we were still congratulating ourselves that such an enormous number of passengers representing various areas of occupations and professions traveled such a long distance and in the confines of Pullman cars, without a single discordant or untoward event. There were hundreds of people on that train. It was a gigantic undertaking, demanding skillful planning, persistence, and dedication on the part of the Brotherhood, and its success was achieved by the cooperation of all the locals and ladies' auxiliaries in the United States and Canada.

The subjects discussed at the convention sessions were exhaustive and productive. Much was accomplished in every phase of organized labor. Each night of the week there was entertainment for the delegates and their friends and citizens of the community, and a magnificent reception and dance on the final night. The local committee provided sight-seeing tours through the beautiful sections of the city and suburbs and Hollywood. The offices and delegates had to be present at each session when I called the roll, but non-delegates and visitors went to call on relatives and friends in Los Angeles, San Francisco, and other places, such as Mexico.

While at the convention, I received word that the Denver Division would consider it an honor if, on my return to Washington, I would stop over and visit them. I agreed. Speaking for the Washington Division delegation, which numbered about 15 porters and their wives, one of the men said to me, "Sister Tucker, if there's no one to meet you at the Denver station, you're going straight back to Washington with us." When we arrived at the station, everyone got off the car with me, and one of them, Mrs. Elizabeth Craig, shouted, "Is there anyone here to meet Sister Tucker?"

Seemingly from nowhere, through the dark, immediately came a loud "Yeah!" It was too funny for words. So I spoke at Denver, then rested in Chicago for a few days, and then I returned to Washington, DC..

In the spring of 1954,, I went on a nationwide tour in behalf of the Auxiliary. The women in many of the local auxiliaries had never seen the International President or Secretary-Treasurer. They heard from Sister Wilson and from me by mail, but Mr. Randolph thought it would be profitable if one of us could go through the country to encourage the members, inform them of union matters, and spur them on to greater efforts.

My meetings were to be both with the men of the Brotherhood and with the women of the Auxiliary. I would have a "family talk", especially if the group was small. We had to build the auxiliaries up. Instead of standing at a lectern, I would sit in a chair and ask them to sit around me and just talk. Mr. Randolph was quite impressed with that.

I was given a send-off banquet in Boston on May 21, which was attended by Brother Randolph as well as Brother Milton Webster, the International Vice President from Chicago. I left Boston for Buffalo and stayed there about two days. In my report, I noted, "The meetings in Boston were fairly attended by the porters and their wives and I think that with a little more encouragement and intensive work by members of the auxiliary themselves, the membership could be noticeably increased...However, it is my understanding that some race-horse activities are conducted at their headquarters, which is distasteful to many who come to meetings...Sister Avery is doing quite nicely with the *Buffalo* auxiliary, and hopes to do better because of my visit, as I was able to clarify some of our rules and give suggestions for activities...Here, some members have been too strait-laced about some types of drinks served at their entertainments. My statement in the matter was that to serve beer with meals should be acceptable to all."

I then traveled to New York City, where I held meetings. I was known pretty well there, of course. The men outnumbered the women in attendance. Although I reported that "my message was received with enthusiasm", I noted "there is a woeful lack of interest shown in the auxiliary by the women, due, I am told, to lack of leadership."

From New York, I went to Jersey City and Newark. Newark was a very strong place for the Brotherhood and Auxiliary. From there I went to Philadelphia, where there was a very strong auxiliary and we had a very fine meeting. I was then supposed to journey to Baltimore, but I had been there so often that Brother Randolph thought it would not be necessary for me to go there again. So, coming through Washington, I went to hold meetings in Richmond and then in Norfolk, Virginia. The numbers there were small. I called on the phone every woman on my roster (I carried my cards from the files with me), yet only nine attended. There were only six present in Norfolk. Then I returned home to Washington for two weeks to rest and pack lighter clothes for a trip to the South.

My first stop was Asheville, North Carolina, where I visited the very fine auxiliary there. The women were so very enthusiastic and progressive. Meetings were held in Atlanta towards the end of June, and from there I went to I then visited Montgomery and Birmingham in Alabama.

When I arrived at Montgomery, Alabama on July 3, Mrs. Nixon, the wife of the president of the local chapter, and a delegation of auxiliary members met me at the station. Mr. Nixon[89] was not due home from work until the next day. I was a guest in their home. Mr. Nixon had built a strong local in Montgomery and he was known in every area of its activities. Everybody knew that he was a strong organized labor man. He talked Brotherhood all over the city. He urged all citizens to contend for their rights and boldly to seek the right to vote—to have no fear or anybody or any agency to hold them back. He preached it all over Montgomery, how the humble porter, by uniting and working fearlessly for recognition, got that recognition and

---

[89] Edgar Daniel Nixon (1899-1987) President both of the Montgomery branch of the Brotherhood as well as the local chapter of the NAACP.

won a contract with the Pullman Company when everybody else said that it could not be done. Mr. Nixon was instrumental in organizing the famous bus strike a few months later, which in many ways was the beginning of the civil rights struggle of the 50s and 60s. When the "strike" was urged, the citizens of Montgomery were already physically, mentally, and spiritually conditioned to carry the boycott to its conclusion., so when Dr. Martin Luther King entered the struggle, he had a firm foundation of citizens to build upon, which led to his success.

While I was in Montgomery, two white labor officials called on me. These two women were interested in our success as women labor organizers. With the Nixons I was invited to a garden party, a brilliant affair, where I met many of Montgomery's black business and professional men and women.

When I arrived at Montgomery, Mr. Nixon found out that in order for me to get to Jacksonville, Florida, my next stop, I would have to ride on a Jim Crow car on the train and then get off and take a bus. The Jim Crow coaches were dirty, smelly, and roachy. He said, "I'm not going to let the New York office bawl me out about Sister Tucker. I'm going to see about a plane for her." So, when my meetings in Montgomery were over, we drove seven miles to the airport. They had no space at the time. If there were cancellations, they told the president, they would let him know. We had just returned to the house when the phone rang. They had a cancellation. We drove back and got the ticket and the next day I flew to Jacksonville. I noted, "I have always considered it very foolish for anyone to travel by air, but I did just that."

From Jacksonville I went on to Tampa and then to a place called Lakeland, where there were lakes all over the city—it was well-named! There was much fruit growing there. I stayed in Tampa with Ella Johnson, a member of the International Executive Board. Her yard was full of lime and grapefruit trees that seemed to bloom year round. So used were the inhabitants to it that the fruit meant little to them. I went on to Columbus, Georgia and Savannah, and then flew to Columbia, South Carolina and Florence, South Carolina, and then home again on July 20. I did all this without riding one of those segregated trains which were the bane of Negro travelers in those days. Although these were standard throughout the South in those days, I never in my life had to ride on one. I would always travel in a roomette. I had everything there that was necessary except for food. I would go to the dining car for meals and there I encountered no discrimination. I have been seated at table with white guests.

It had been a very good trip for me, and it was helpful to those I visited. I was able to sit down like one of them and talk about things they appreciated. Many times they would give a dinner or some other kind of social affair for me, and on one occasion, I was treated to a boat trip down the Savannah River. It was an education to me because I had never been so far South and I was surprised that I did not encounter a single unpleasant racial incident and I was amazed at how well the Negroes lived. The porters owned fine homes (at least so far as I could see) and there was not one in which I lodged that was not comfortable and attractive. The porters were making money now and the salary was the same all over the land. Since the cost of living is or was less in the South, the porters there had more to gain.

I was supposed to go west for a similar trip, but Sister Wilson became ill and I had to return to do some of the work that she was unable to do at the time. On October 20 I was given a huge testimonial banquet in Baldwin Hall at Howard University.

Reflecting on the trip, I wrote: "I am convinced that we are still a race of children and that we have to be told the same thing over and over again before a statement is comprehended and accepted as fat. In other words, we must be taught constantly. My talks with the men and women of the zone covered the simple reasons for our Union of both the men and the women. Every group I addressed, even in the well established locals, told me that they had...learned more about the organization than ever before. Of course, they had heard before, but forgotten. My concern is, "Have we failed along the line" to stress over and over again the simple, everyday, down to earth reasons for our organization, our benefits, its obligations, its fees, taxes, and assessments? Have we failed to press indelibly upon the minds of our adherents the spiritual side of our Union, that side which binds us together that when we are called, we answer the call. For instance, in some places I visited, officials stated that they received word from headquarters that there would be meetings, but they didn't know what "it was all about." My answer to them was that they were to come to find out what "it was all about." I stated emphatically that whatever word came from headquarters should be considered as an 'order' and the fundamental asset of Labor is to obey official 'orders,' for much can be gained or lost if orders are or are not carried through.

"In many places, I was told that the men would turn out in full numbers if they knew that there was to be a discussion of a raise in salary or a change in 'runs', but for nothing else.

"I found, especially among our women, that some consider themselves better than others to the extent that they refuse to join the auxiliary. Of course, my talks covered this item and all of the items I have mentioned above and the ones to follow. In some instances, these wives try to influence other women against joining the auxiliary. We have some Pullman wives who feel superior to train porters' wives. We still have to cope with the porter who does not want his wife to join. Our men, as a whole, have married women of superior ability and our Union needs their intelligence and ability to build the morale of our men and also to build a stronger union. We need them and their intelligence for leadership purposes, but such leadership must be a devoted, unselfish leadership.

"In some of our auxiliaries, especially in some parts of the South, the opening of the meetings is patterned after the opening of a church service—with devotional services. This is true in Birmingham and Montgomery and maybe one or two others. Of course, I have no special quarrel with this, but, I do think that is a differentiation that should be made in this particular instance, to start with, so that proper differentiation will be made between Union lines and other organizational lines.

"I have found conflict between members of the auxiliaries as to types of entertainments. Some of our women object to dances and activities at which alcoholic beverages are sold. My suggestion was that the auxiliary program should be so varied as to satisfy the desires of all.

A sermon in a church or pew rally for all who can help do so; or dinners, suppers and card parties with the serving of beverages when it is not against the law or the good name of the Brotherhood.

"In some districts, there were members of the Brotherhood and Auxiliary who were neglecting their meetings but spending much time actually meeting with and working for the NAACP and secret organizations and taking part in and contributing to many church activities while they could not attend Brotherhood or Auxiliary meetings once or twice a month. These people have not the proper perspective. I discussed this in my talks...

"As I see it, our auxiliaries, especially our smaller auxiliaries, need closer supervision. In many instances they are working in the dark, so to speak. One way to strengthen them other than visits by officials is that as many members as possible visit other auxiliaries near them. This can be accomplished because most of our members have cars, thus, Birmingham could visit Montgomery, Tampa, Jacksonville, and Tampa, Lakeland; Baltimore, Philadelphia; Jersey City and New York and vice versa."

"I made a number of recommendations, including "that copies of the three Brotherhood songs, 'Hold the Fort,' 'I Shall Not Be Moved,' and 'John Brown's Body' be printed and sent to all the Locals, especially the Southern auxiliaries as opening and closing songs, since these are our Labor songs. That a simple opening with the Chaplain's prayer and our Labor songs be the procedure before the regular business.

"That the *Birmingham* and *Montgomery* locals, men and women, be sent copies of our Brotherhood songs immediately, so that the opening of their meetings can be in the Labor tradition and not the tradition of a church service, as I found it.

"Since the New York auxiliary has gone from bad to worse because of the members' dissatisfaction with its leadership, the president; and since interest is almost completely lost; since just four or five stalwart are remaining with the hope that a change will be made, and since the president is said to be devoid of leadership qualities, unprepared, uncouth, and vindictive, I recommend that, in the interest of the International Ladies Auxiliary and the International Brotherhood of Sleeping Car Porters, the New York Ladies' Auxiliary be dissolved immediately and reorganized with the hope that with a new start, progress can be made, for the New York Auxiliary should be a shining example to all other auxiliaries.

"That for the good of the Boston Local and Auxiliary in particular and the Brotherhood in general, that the Boston headquarters be investigated regarding race horse activities.

"That a statement be drafted to the effect that every Porter's wife and other female members of his family are required and requested to join the Ladies Auxiliary because in the auxiliaries all types of abilities can be used, that where some may excel in one category, others may excel in another. We have need for these several abilities in the further development of the Brotherhood.

"That each Auxiliary and Local plan types of programs and activities so varied that they will appeal to various members.

"That a strong statement be made regarding the members of the various Locals and Auxiliaries for neglecting to attend their own meetings, that their first specific interest must be in the Brotherhood."

"That the International arrange programs for the Locals and Auxiliaries so that the meetings will be inviting and the program attractive. That there be a tie-in with the men to their Union and a tie-in with the auxiliary program. This, of course, should bring the men and women in the Worker's Education orbit.

"That a code be set up for Local Counselors, so that they may have a clear idea of the duties of that office. Such a code would set forth the fact that it is not the office of a dictator but an official who has studied the rules of the

Auxiliary and who has the ability to advise in the true spirit of the Brotherhood."

I continued as International Secretary-Treasurer of the Ladies Auxiliary until it passed out of existence when I was well into my eighties, due to the falling off of the railroads. I attended what was to be the last convention in Chicago in 1971. I took a plane there, but. although I was then 90, I came back by train, because I believed that it would be for the last time on my favorite form of transportation. Companies are trying to get rid of passenger service now, but I think passenger railroad service is vital t this country. Besides, I have always loved the train, ever since I was a little girl, and would much rather travel by rail than by air.

The Brotherhood served a great and vital purpose in its day. Not only did it elevate the standard of living for the Pullman porters, it was instrumental in bringing about civil rights legislation. It was also an education to its members, as so many had little or no formal schooling. Mr. Randolph was able to raise their level of confidence and self-esteem. Because of the Brotherhood, many realized their potential. I think it is marvelous that our organization, which was "just dug up", as Brother Randolph said, flourished for half a century and accomplished so much good.

Chapter XXI--Senior Citizen

As I entered my late seventies, I lost what remained of my family. My last surviving sister, Marietta Clinkscales Alexander, had fallen upon very hard times. She had been living in Southeast with a family whose children she instructed in music. As she approached eighty, her eyesight failed and she had to be moved to the Stoddard Baptist Home, where our Grandmother Thompson had spent the last years of her life. Although she was blind, Marietta continued to play the piano at the religious services at the home. She vowed to play the piano as long as she lived as "a living memorial" to our father who had trained her. I visited Marietta regularly and did what I could to make her happy. I took care of all her business and paid her bills. Whenever possible, I would send her a dress or something useful from a far-off place when I happened to have traveled. The other inmates would see these gifts and, for days, they were topics of discussion at the Home.. Marietta took pride in showing them what her sister had sent her. Once, one of the matrons asked, "Mrs. Tucker, how are you feeling?" and I answered that I wasn't feeling well. Marietta overheard and pleaded with me, "Now, Rose don't you dare die now! I don't know what I would do without you!"

One time I told her that my doctor had advised me to lose weight. When I was young, people didn't have the aversion to fat that they do today. I have never weighed less than 185 in my adult life. Now my doctor said I was too heavy. Marietta begged me not to diet. "You need your weight. Weight gives you strength." So, I listened to my sister and not the doctor, and am none the worse for it.

Marietta died in the early morning of January 25, 1959. The previous night she had refused to go to bed, and the nurse could not persuade her to lie down. Finally, while standing, she slid to the floor, dead. She seemed to have had no pain. She would have been 84 if she had lived to April.

I never thought of Berthea as an old man, but he was 80[90] in 1958. He had long since retired and now he sat around a lot. We got along better. As always, he trusted me. Nobody could make him believe anything adverse about me, but he still groused and complained. Because of his 35 years of service to the Pullman Company, and his irregular sleeping and eating habits, Berthea's digestion was so impaired that I had to select and prepare his food carefully. Having traveled through so many changes of climate during a 20 or more hour run, he, as well as other porters, suffered chronic colds. He had three major surgeries in his later

---

[90] According to the census of 1880, he would have been 80 in 1956.

years. When he was hospitalized the first time, I would go to work and stay till 12:45, then drive to Freedmen's Hospital and stay until three, then go back to work until 6:45, and then return to the hospital to stay until visiting hours were over at eight. I procured a practical nurse to stay with him from eight until four. When he got home, however, he complained, "My wife never does anything for me."

In 1961 it was apparent that his health was fast failing.[91] After consultation with several doctors, he entered the Washington Hospital Center for medication and surgery. I had long since given up driving the car, so, to visit him, I had to use public transportation, transferring twice on earth trip. I would arrive at the hospital at 11 o'clock in the morning and remain with him until after 5 o'clock in the evening. It was dark and very cold those days in December when I left the hospital for home, and, arriving home, I had to prepare my dinner and do the many chores around the house.

Surgery was performed on Berthea on December 6. I was in his room when he was brought in after the operation. I visited him every day the three weeks he was confined, but one. Thursday, December 28 I had developed such a cold that I was advised to take medication and remain in bed for

---

[91] Mrs. Tucker said Berthea suffered from colon cancer.

the day. On Friday morning, as I was preparing for my visit to Berthea, the doctor called from the hospital and asked, "Mrs. Tucker, are you alone?"

"Yes, I am," I replied.

As gently as he could, he said, "Your husband has just died."

It was December 29, 1961. Berthea was 83 years old. I was 80. Friends and neighbors were very kind to me. Berthea's nephew, Joseph Smith, and his wife Ethel, came from Springfield, Massachusetts to be with me, as did another of his nephew's wives, Mary Smith, from Pittsburgh, Pennsylvania. The Brotherhood local turned out in full at the funeral services which were held at the Fifteenth Street Presbyterian Church, of which Berthea had been a member for years before I met him. The burial was in the family plot in the old Harmony Cemetery in Washington,

I was sorrowful when Berthea died, but I did not allow myself to sink to the depth of sorrow as when Poet died. It was because of the lasting lesson I learned from Mrs. Dunlap's words of wisdom when she visited me years before, words which not only comforted me, but sustained me and challenged me to carry on.

I had nursed Berthea through two previous operations, therefore I was very sad at his death, for I had done everything within my knowledge to keep him alive and well, and I had gladly made many sacrifices, spiritual, physical, and financial, that he might be happy. But I failed. There were so many blessings he had that he failed to enjoy or even recognize, and there were many more for him had he only reached out for them. As I look back over the 43 years I was Berthea's wife, I am conscious of the adjustment I had to make . Most of the time I drove him to work and met him with the car to bring him home. I had to adjust to his severity towards me and lack of sensitivity for my well-being and my efforts in making the house a home. His lack of communication and his unwillingness to confide in me and his failure to share with me deeply distressed me. I received no encouragement for my interest in the BSCP, a union whose purpose was to improve his working conditions, as well as those of all the other porters, and to increase the paycheck to an adequate wage, commensurate to work performed. My chagrin was eased by prayer for patience and understanding and by taking several vacations without leaving the city. Yet I have always appreciated the fact that Berthea had explicit faith in my integrity under all circumstances.

Often, as I sit here alone, I miss him and wish he were back, sitting in his rocking chair, as was the custom of his later years. But then I realize he would be scolding and complaining and I think that it is just as well that he is not here. He had great affection for me, but he never showed it. He believed that a man should make it hard on a woman. "You've got to show your wife who's boss!" But he really loved me. It was if he could strip everything away from me but my basic self, everything would have been all right. But he felt threatened whenever I accomplished anything, so deep was his inferiority complex. A friend of mine once interpreted the situation with Mr. Tucker: "He's down there. You're up here. You bring him up so far and he feels out of place and he drops back again." Maybe that was the way it was.

As I look back, I do not know how I managed to make out, but I know that my marriage with Mr. Tucker was to be. I have been led into things I could not get out of. God was in the whole thing. My life was broader (although not better) with Mr. Tucker than with Dr. Corrothers.

Because of what I have been through, out of it has come something which has enlightened me. I have been able to use this knowledge to help a great number of people. When people in distress have come, I was able to say, "What you have been through, I have been through."

My pastor, Dr. Robert P. Johnson, successor to Dr. Taylor, once asked me, "Are you sorry you married Mr. Tucker?"

I replied, "No. It was in the cards." In other words, it was God's plan and His will for me.

I told him,"It seems that my life has never been wholly under my control, but under the command of a higher power which constrained me toward a series of acts which I had not planned or contemplated." One can work beyond a thing that pierces the heart. God will free us to overcome the pain and transcend it to accomplish His good purpose. In retrospect, marrying Berthea opened up for me a broader sphere of operation, which in time, afforded me the opportunity to touch the lives of many hundreds of men and women in the United States of America and parts of Canada.

The recent years have not been uneventful. In 1967, when I was 86, I was hospitalized with anaemia, but recovered in time to give the severance address for my pastor, Dr. Robert P. Johnson, who was resigning to accept a position as Moderator of the New York Presbytery. This I did just three days after being discharged from the hospital. At the end of my delivery I was given a standing ovation. In a few days, I received a request from the Presbytery for a copy of my address. I sent it and it was reproduced and copies sent to all the Presbyterian churches in the area.

In my late 80s I was taken ill with pneumonia. After my recovery, I thought it best to give up my home and reside in the Roosevelt for Senior Citizens. So I put my home up for sale, gave away most of my furniture, and went to live in the hotel. The Roosevelt was located in a very attractive part of the city, and its distinctive environment was much to be desired. However, in a few days, I found many things undesirable. The longer I stayed, however, the less I liked it. There was a coldness on the part of the staff. The waitresses were rude to the guests, not only in action, but in speech. We were constantly afraid of being scalded by their careless manner of handling the pitchers of hot water for our tea. The food was virtually slammed on the table to us.

    I was in the lobby one day and met a friend, Miss Louise Madella, who had just moved in. I had known her for years. She was well educated, cultured, and an avid reader. She had traveled to many of the well-known capitals of the world. At dinner one evening Miss Madella asked for more hot water for her tea. The waitress, an African, caustically retorted, "That's the trouble with you blacks. You think too much of yourselves." This outburst included all of us in the room who were black. The waitress herself was black. Why the enmity? Was it the difference in status—that of a guest and waitress, or is there a deep-seated hatred in the African heart against the American black? I hope neither is true for the sake of all of us.

    A white woman came to my table one morning and said, "This is the third table I've been to and they won't serve me." I asked her how long she had been here. "Four years," she said. I asked her if she had complained. She said she had many times and it had done no good.

"Why do you remain here?" I asked.

"Because I have no place else to go."

I could hear that statement over and over again: "I have no place else to go." This expression of helplessness and hopelessness saddened me.

One Saturday night I had eaten my dinner and, on leaving the dining room, I passed the next group going in to eat. This long line of aged people reminded me of that passage of Scripture which reads, "And they brought to Him the lame, the halt, and the blind." This was the most depressing scene in the world for me to gaze on—this long line of bending forms, both black and white, this veritable sea of canes, crutches, walkers, and wheelchairs. I decided to return to my home after remaining in the hotel for less than a month. I learned much of life and its tragedies in that hotel. My short tenure there gave an aspect of life as it is lived that I never witnessed before.

So even though I had paid two months rent, I returned to my home. My friends said, "You just didn't want to be around those old people." I feel that God wanted me to return to my home. I felt that this was indicated by the fact that when I returned, I found that my basement was flooded.

Had this gone unattended much longer, the house would have been severely damaged. So I have been very content in my decision. I had luckily retained enough furniture to make for a comfortable existence. I now live entirely on the first floor, since my physicians have advised me against climbing the stairs. I live alone. My neighborhood is deteriorating. Until the 1930s, we were the only black family, but all that has now changed. Twice my house has been broken into, but thankfully, I have been asleep at the time and have not been hurt. One morning I awoke and found the doors open and my television and radio gone. I feel that God wanted me to sleep through the robbery. Had I awakened to find burglars in my house, I might have cried out or struggled, and, as a result been injured or killed. So I just trust in God that He will take care of me and I try not to be afraid.

  Except for several trips to Canada in connection with the Brotherhood,, I had never been out of the country until the summer of 1972, when, at 90, I went on a cruise to the Bahamas with friends. We went to Baltimore by limousine and flew to Miami, whence we took the cruise ship. One evening the two men in charge of the affair asked "Mrs. Tucker" to come forward. Standing on either side of me, they told the group, "Here is a passenger who is 90 years old." Everyone applauded and both men, who were white, kissed me. For the rest of the cruise, people would come and say, "Why, you don't look like you're 90. You haven't a wrinkle." One white woman came to me in the powder room and said, "I can't believe you are 90. I am just 69 and I have many more wrinkles than you. May I kiss you?" One young man in evening dress came to me and asked me to dance with him. He was only about 25 or 30. I thanked him, but told him I do not dance.

I do not have too much sympathy for today's feminism. One of the sins of slavery was that it separated husband from wife and parents from children. I think the result of that is shown today in that colored men don't seem to feel the necessity of taking their places as men and taking care of their families. It all comes from slavery, and I think that we must go back and continue to work towards the training of our sons. It's up to the "new generation" to train their sons to take on their full responsibility. This is one reason why I am not in favor of "Women's Lib."

I had an occasion in my church one Sunday, not long ago, to speak up because there were two white women from the Presbytery there, one of them a Presbyterian minister's wife, and, oh, my, she was one of these "Women's Libbers." She didn't even use her husband's name! She wanted to use her maiden name. After she spoke in behalf of Women's Liberation, I got up. I have never been afraid to speak up. I have to speak out. I would despise myself if I did not. I said, "I want to be as *kind* as I can, but we have a different culture than yours. We know that we must stand by *our* husbands. We can't afford to lessen their manhood. Slavery did that. By working together, we have educated our children that they have a better existence."

Another woman in the audience asked, "What do you want us to do, leave our husbands?"

Then I said, "We must stand together. *We* feel the necessity to support *our* husbands, that they can be strong and so that they will know that they are men in every sense!"

Oh, she turned red in the face! Afterwards, they served some refreshments and I was witting on the other side of the church when the other speaker came up and said, "Mrs. Tucker, I know just how you feel."

I said to her, "Oh, no, you *don't!*" I didn't give any quarter. "You can't know how we feel because you're not black! You don't know what we've been through! You may try to understand, but you'll never understand!"

Oh, this lady was embarrassed! But we are different, no matter what you say. We have a different background, and I think it is good that we are different.

It's a complex situation in the United States today and I think the reason that things are in the condition they are now in is because of President Nixon's attitude towards the poor. [This was 1975]. Nixon didn't get many votes from colored people. Somehow or other, colored people instinctively feared that he wouldn't do well towards them. And when they didn't vote for him, why, he began to take reprisals on black people and try to close up all the agencies that helped colored people. I've always said that God only lets folks go so far. I make people laugh when I say, "Don't fool with God's niggers!" With us black people God only lets folks go so far. Now Nixon thought that he was just going to do as he felt with black people. It was a nigger that found him out. This guard was attending to his business and he noticed that a door was taped. He noticed it and called the officers. Few people will give that man credit for opening up this whole thing. As a result, he lost his job, and, instead of getting a better job, he couldn't get any. Of course, black people commenced to raise Cain about it and I think he has something now. Now, when I was a young girl there was a policeman—I can't think of his first name, but he was a West—who arrested a president. The President was on his horse and drove his horse over one of the lawns and this policeman saw him *and arrested him.* It was one of the public lawns. And, do you know, that man was *complimented* and given a lifetime job, who had the nerve to arrest a president. And now this man was the cause of thieves being arrested and instead of being credit for it, he was punished for it. Those are the things that black people are thinking about. They knew instinctively that Nixon was not going to be a good president. And that's a thing that I don't understand, that there is something very strange how God works with us as a people. I don't think it's so much that we are better, but it may be that we are so oppressed that God works in that manner to relieve us of that oppression.

Now our young people have the attitude of taking nothing and the powers that be will just have to reckon with them. We had some older people who used to say, "Well, just let God do this," and "God will do that." I believe that, too, but I believe we've got to let God help us by doing what we can. I think that we as a race have power and that we are now using it, and as our youngsters become more interested in racial affairs, and become *more identified* with the race, we will find that there will be conflicts if some changes are not made. Our youngsters are not afraid like they were when I was young. Their parents are not afraid. The black youngsters are willing to suffer in order that we can get what are our rights. We are reminded that the black people made this country what it is. Often in the South the colored men did the flowers, they did the planting, they did the reaping, they did the sewing and the quilting and everything to make the lives of those people bearable and pleasant, and in turn they were deprived of those benefits. Now they have race pride enough to say, "No longer will we be second class citizens." As a result of their working together and understanding the situation, we have a fine group of men and women who are demanding recognition and black women and black men are getting into positions of influence and we're going to continue to do that.[92]

---

[92] The remarks on feminism and on race Mrs. Tucker edited out of her work, and are restored unvarnished and unsmoothed. In terms of the language and expression, those paragraphs, more than any other, are vintage and unexpurgated Rosina Tucker!

Epilogue

Having dealt with various groups of people, unpleasant occurrences have ensued which at the moment caused me some concern, but, on reflection I accepted such as challenges and used what ability I had to surmount them, rather than allow them to depress me, for I have grown to the degree that I have no fear of adverse opinions. Trying to agree with everyone, I would find myself going around in circles. So, instead of circling, trying to please many, I am still using my experiences, serving the best I can when I am needed, in spite of adverse opinions.

.I have found myself working with individuals who had attended schools of higher education, whose posture was that of superiority to all around them, magnified by their exalting themselves and denigrating others not so fortune. On the other hand, I have worked with those who took pride in their ignorance, designating scholars as "educated fools."I have, however, the blessing to have known and worked with intellectuals as well as the unlettered, who were delightful, compassionate, unassuming, and gracious, whose hearts vibrated with serene rhythm with my heart and the hearts of all who knew them.

There are many elderly people who object to telling their age and who pretend to be younger than they are. I have never been inclined to do so. The year after Berthea died, my last surviving cousin, Eva Harvey Blake, a retired high school teacher, died at 86. I was called to testify in court concerned matters relating to her estate. Also called to testify was an old friend of Eva's who went to school with her and began teaching at the same time that Eva did. I chuckled when she was asked her age and she replied timidly, "Seventy." When I took the stand and was asked my age, I shocked everybody by saying, loudly and clearly, "I am eighty years old." Indeed, especially as time goes by, I find my age, far from a disadvantage, an actual asset.

Often I have to transact business and have to give my age. I am seldom believed.[93] At times I will say, "Now, you know a woman never puts up her age, rather she will lower it." This statement usually convinces them. Then others are called around me, and, on being told my age, they invariably will say, "God bless you." When I was preparing for an eye operation in January, 1975, a clerk from the hospital called me to set the time. She asked my full name and age, and I gave her my name and said to her that she would not believe my age. She said that she would believe any age I gave. When I said that I was 93 years old, she said, "What year

---

[93] She wrote this in her late 90s.

were you born?" I said, "I told you that you would not believe me, and now you want me to prove it."

The subject of my age becomes rather amusing at times. I was trying to hail a cab one day to take me to the doctor's office for my regular monthly appointment. I had not been successful when one of my neighbors, Joseph Murray, came by. Realizing my plight, he stopped a police car and told the officer therein, "Here's a lady almost 100 years old and she can't get a cab." At once, one of the officers got out of the scout car and stopped the first cab in sight, although it was heading in the opposite direction. The officer stopped traffic and motioned him to cross the highway and take me to my destination, saying, "This woman is almost 100 years old." At first the cabbie seemed disturbed, but he soon recovered and began questioning me concerning general conditions when I was young. He was anxious to know if boys and girls smoked and drank then as they do now. My answer was, "No, it was a disgrace for a girl to smoke or drink." He asked if children were as rude and disobedient to their parents as they are now. My answer was, "By no means." He asked if girls became pregnant as they do now. My answer was, "This was not as prevalent then as now, but, whereas girls are more brazen now, then they were hidden during their pregnancy, for during those years many girls never outlived their disgrace."

I am frequently asked to what I attribute my long life.[94] My reply is that I had not thought too much about age until my sister Marietta reached her seventy-fifth birthday and exclaimed, "Just to think I am three quarters of a century old!" It was then that I wondered if I would reach that age. However, my reply to the question is that I have no answer, only to say that my life is in God's hands and that He has a purpose for me, and I shall live until His purpose is fulfilled. Everybody's life has a purpose—even my brothers and sisters who died as babies—they had a purpose too, and they fulfilled it. Therefore, I must pursue that purpose. I have not spared myself in the interest of my home, my church, and the community or with individuals and groups of various professions and occupations, and I shall continue to do so, for remembering the past, faith directs me to welcome the future.

I think there's a great need for Christ in the world today, a great need. I think that is one of our weaknesses as a race. We have gone away from Christ. I think that one of the reasons for it is that so many who claim to be Christians don't act like Christians, and our youngsters are more realistic today. They want to see action with your beliefs. Our parents believed in God and although they couldn't read

---

[94] Mrs. Tucker speculated that her longevity may have been the result of living most of her life indoors and being spared exposure to the elements.

or write, there was that deep belief, and although they were slaves they knew that they would be delivered.. They said it. They told their children, "It may not be in our day, but *we will be free.*" That was the Spirit of God breathing that fact into them. I feel that God is working today, and all we've got to do is *listen to His voice,* and try. None of us are perfect. We can try to do the right thing. We may find ourselves separated from people who believe as we do, but I think that God is working today and in His time He will bring these things around. But as a people we will have to get back to a belief in God.

I don't know all the Bible, so I can't say I believe in it all, but I do believe our confession that Christ was the Son of God and He came down in the flesh to redeem us that we may have everlasting life. Now there may be a whole lot about that which I do not understand, but that is my basic belief and I think that is required of all of us. There are many, many things in the Bible that I do not understand, but I try to understand what I can. I wouldn't dare discuss a whole lot of things.

Throughout my long life, the guiding force has been my faith in God. I have not had an easy life. After all, I lost everybody: two husbands, my only son, my sisters, my brothers, my mother and my father. There have been times when I just needed spiritual help and I found it in God. I had a favorite couch in my dining room which Berthea later said was dilapidated and threw away, but, while we had it, it was my "praying place." I would get down there and meditate and think. I call it communicating, or rather, the Spirit communicating with me. In this way, the Holy Spirit has helped me and encouraged me.

Then, sometimes He led me to seek the help of other Christians. When Dr. Taylor was at Fifteenth Street Church, I would go to him frequently for counsel. I would drive to his home at First and S Streets. I would say, "Reverend Taylor, I just want to talk to you so you can help me with my thinking." He was a great help to me and many times he came to me with problems concerning the church and I would try to help him.

But there are times when one needs reassurance. Even though I have had great faith since I was twelve years old, there are times when one's faith weakens a bit under great stress. Then one needs someone to help one think it out, and this is how Dr. Taylor often helped me. One time he said, "Mrs. Tucker, stand still and see the salvation of the Lord!" Now, when things come to me, when things do not happen as I would want them to, I say it is simply that I need patience and need to rely upon someone beyond myself. Many times I will pray, "God, help me to see evidences of Your care!"

We are told to love God, and sometimes in my prayers, I have said, "God, I don't know whether I love you acceptably or not. Just help me to love You in the way you'd have me to do." One has to confess one's weaknesses. The only way one can be strong, is to confess one's weakness.

I feel that the hand of God was present in many of the things that happened in my life. I feel that He compelled me to come to Washington after Dr. Corrothers died. I tried to remain in West Chester, but kept falling ill. I feel that He was behind my marriage to Mr. Tucker. I have been led to do so many things that previously I had no intention of doing. I have left this house to go one place and have found myself going in another direction, and, when I got there, I found that this is where I was supposed to be at the time.

I am not saying, "Death, come and get me," but I know that an end of my earthly existence before very long is a distinct possibility. I hope I will be reconciled to death when it does come. I cannot say that I am afraid, but it is something one knows not know about and one is always anxious about something one does not know about. But I expect to go wherever Christ is, and I expect that is heaven. Although I have not thought too much about it, I trust it will be there that I will see again all of those I have loved here but lost. But I do not think too much about it. If God has taken care of me through all my life here, he will take care of the eternal matters, too. One must let things take care of themselves. One must trust. But I feel our greatest effort should be to live right here on earth. I think one thing that is needed in this world is a greater spirituality. People need a trusting relationship with Christ. This is indispensable for a peaceable society. On that note, I will close my life story.

People often ask me, "What was it like in your day?" I replied, "*Today* is my day just as it is your day!" Although I live far removed from the time I was born, I do not feel that my heart should dwell in the past. It is in the future. Each day added to another has culminated in growth that has led to my present experience and made me the person I am today and will be tomorrow.

As I survey the Spring, the Summer, the Fall and the Winter of my life, with its illness and health, poverty and wealth, envy and goodwill, triumphs and defeats and life and death, I can but conclude that these incidents form the weave and woof of the texture of the fabric of my being, challenging me and urging me to my ultimate emotional and spiritual fulfillment. Thus, while I live, let not my life be in vain, and when I depart, may there be at times remembrances of me and My Life as I Have Lived It.

Afterword

Mother Tucker

When Rosina Tucker finished her drafts of her autobiography in or around 1978, she still had a decade to live, and these years were among the most productive of her life.

Several years before, she spoke at the church of which I was pastor at the time. I wrote in my diary: "Mrs. Tucker stood at the altar to speak and read a very heartfelt talk about what her favorite hymns meant to her. Her voice was feeble, but audible, her delivery halting, but effective. Would that I had a tape recorder. She gave me a very flattering introduction and talked about my father & aunts." As the years went on, she was more and more in demand as a speaker.

Around the time of her hundredth birthday, she narrated an hour long television documentary "Miles of Smiles" about the Brotherhood of Sleeping Car Porters. Film-maker Paul Wagner recalled, "We thought it would be a film with all men in it since they were the ones who were the Pullman porters. Then we met Mrs. Tucker...[and] we were immediately struck by her amazing personal strength.

She was just so powerful the way she expressed herself. Her power was so compelling that a simple cameo appearance in the half hour film turned into a job narrating an hour long documentary."[95] Tucker also commented, "Her role was vital, but not really appreciated in the 1930s, not only because she was black, but also because she was a woman."[96]

In her tenth decade she was discovered by folklorists, and recruited to speak at the Smithsonian Folklife Festival. "Audiences just love her," commented Marjorie Hunt, a folklorist at the Smithsonian. "They'll sit in rapt attention. She is a living treasure."[97] Usually accompanied by her friend, Norma McDaniel, she traveled around the country, talking mostly about the genesis of the Brotherhood of Sleeping Car Porters.

Mother Tucker was in demand as a speaker in schools throughout the Washington area. "I tell them about the studies [when she was a girl] and how children dressed and talked. I tell them different things about myself, how I came in contact [with various people].[98] On two occasions

---

[95] *Washington Times*, March 4, 1987

[96] *Washington Post*, March 12, 1987

[97] *Washington Post*, November 3, 1986

[98] Ibid.

she agreed to speak to my students at South Lakes High School in Reston, where I taught history for two and a half decades. In my diary of April 6, 1984, I entered: "I went at 8 [AM] to pick up Mrs. Tucker. She is...much feebler than when I used to go there regularly (that was 10 years ago!). She is almost totally deaf and constantly muttering to herself. Still, she was, I think, pleased to go. Mrs. Norma McDaniel, a retired music teacher, went along. She is Mrs. T's constant traveling companion. Everyone was glad to see her. We wheeled her to the Blue Subschool, where she took an office chair behind a desk. She did not want a microphone, but her voice was weak and the kids in the back had to strain to hear her. She talked about the Union and then about her philosophy of life. It was impressive to hear her fine power of expression and eloquent vocabulary and precise diction—a relic of an age that is past. Several teachers and students asked her questions."

In 1983 Rosina Tucker was honored for her work by the Leadership Council on Civil Rights, which gave her its Hubert H. Humphrey Civil Rights Award. She was interviewed on television and radio shows, as late as the age of 105, when she appeared on the "Phil Donohue Show." At 102, she testified before the Senate sub-committee which was gathering information on aging, and was asked why she thought she lived so long. "Most of my family lived to heir mid-to-late 80s," she told chairman Claiborne Pell. "My great grandmother lived to be 101, my father died in his 50s, and my grandparents lived until their nineties. I don't know why we live so long."[99]

After the age of 100, the birthday of "Mother Tucker" was celebrated at Fifteenth Street Presbyterian Church. A reporter from the *Post* wrote in 1984, "Midway through her 103rd birthday party Sunday, Rosina Tucker went to the piano to play and sing for 200 friends who had gathered at the Fifteenth Street Presbyterian Church. The song was 'November Rose.'"[100] By then, Tucker's once-

---

[99] Mrs. Tucker often attributed her long life to the fact that she was an indoors person and never allowed herself to be "subjected to the elements." S did in fact have relatives who lived to a great age: her mother died at 93, her maternal grandmother at 97. Her paternal grandparents seem to have died young, but her father's maternal grandparents died at 89 and 101 Three of their children lived at least into their 80s. . It is significant that, at least according to her recollections, none of the long-lived members of her family ever suffered from dementia. However, many of her family died young, many of tuberculosis. Her father (who died at 57 of a sudden cardiac arrest) and his siblings were all short-lived (his brother Harry died in his late 30s of tuberculosis; another brother Griffin, died in his early 30s, of an abscess of the pelvis; sister Kate at 32 of tuberculosis and sister Jeanette at 59 of heart disease). Of Rosina Tucker's siblings, only one, her sister Marietta, who died at nearly 84, lived to old age; four died in infancy or early childhood; Ben died at 57 (throat cancer); Jeanette at 47 (a sudden cardiac arrest); and Harry at 42 (tuberculosis). Her only son (who has been described as an inveterate smoker of cigars) died at 45, of lung cancer. Her only nephew lived to 65, but her only niece was past 90 when she died.

[100] *Washington Post*, November 8, 1984

statuesque frame had shrunk to the point that more than one reporter described her as "a tiny woman." She walked erect, steadfastly refusing the use of a cane, but leaning heavily on the arms of a companion. She declared proudly that she still fixed her own breakfast every morning, cleaned her home, and wrote her speeches. She conceded, however, that she wished her body could work as quick as her mind." She declared, "I've been almost every place I ever wanted to go, met many interesting people and basically had a good life. But that doesn't mean I'm ready for the Man to come get me!"[101]

At 104, she participated in a picket of a Safeway near her house in a futile attempt to stop the supermarket from moving out of the area and leaving her neighborhood without an adequate grocery store.

At Mother Tucker's 105th birthday party, a reporter noted, "For the past several years, she has thrown the birthday party for her friends, organizing the affair and hiring the caterer. This year, after she had two minor heart attacks, her friends took over. Tucker was under doctor's orders not to talk, but could not resist addressing the audience of more than a hundred admirers. "I have made many friends in this church and lost many of my friends,"

---

[101] Ibid.

she declared. "I had two heart attacks lately, but the devil hasn't gotten me down yet." She helped conduct a stanza of "Lift Every Voice and Sing." Her physician told the reporter, "For 105, she's doing very well. I see her once a month unless she calls for something else. Everything is house calls because she says she's too old for office visits."

To an almost unique extent, "Mother Tucker" remained physically and mentally vigorous through her 90s. By the time she reached the century mark, her body was beginning to grow feeble, but her mind remained intact to the very end, without the slightest sign of dementia or Alzheimer's.

Shortly after Christmas, 1986, Mrs. Tucker was taken to the Washington Hospital Center. In my diary of January 12, 1987, I wrote: "I went to see Rosina Tucker in the hospital Ctr. She broke a hip...She is unconscious and filled with tubes and cords and wires. Why can't a lady at 105 be allowed to die in peace? That is gruesome. She is truly remarkable and it was a great grace that I was permitted to know her...She is surely the last of the true Victorian ladies."

On February 1, I noted: "I went out to see 'Mother' Tucker. She grabbed my hand and tried desperately to say something, but she couldn't talk because they've put this d___d tube in her throat. The nurses said she's tried to disconnect herself—so they've tied her hands...What a terrible way to end what has been a beautiful life!"

On February 15: "After church I went to see Mrs. Tucker. She seemed no better to me...She still has a tube running into her throat, preventing her from talking. She squeezed my hand and definitely knew me. <u>What</u> she was trying to communicate, I could not say."

The Great Passage came for Rosina Tucker on March 3, 1987. At 105 years and nearly four months, she was described as "the District's oldest resident."[102]

Her funeral on March 9 was at Fifteenth Street Church. I wrote that day: "The church was packed and the funeral was very nice—many musical selections, including the 'Inflammatus',
sung beautifully with a soprano soloist with almost an operatic voice. [John] Pharr [the pastor] preached on 'The Last Word'—on Mrs. Tucker, noting that she always had 'the last word' in any meeting...I read the Epistle & Gospel...A soloist sang 'I Did It My Way', which was quite appropriate for Mrs. Tucker. It was a nice occasion—she was really a wonderful person..."

After she was buried in Harmony Cemetery in the near Maryland suburbs, which I described as "an ugly little

---

[102] *Washington Afro-American*, November 9, 1987

place with no headstones, situated next to a cheap, noisy housing project blaring with cheap music[103]," it started to rain, and someone in the car expressed satisfaction that the storm had held off until after the obsequies. Somebody else commented that she wasn't surprised, because "It's just like Mother Tucker to go up to God and demand, 'Now, don't you *dare* let it rain on my funeral!'"

---

[103] Most of Mrs. Tucker's relatives were buried in the original Harmony Cemetery in Washington, which was dug up in the early 60s and subsequent became a Metro lot. She had the remains of her son transferred to the "New Harmony", where she was buried.

Appendix I-Compensations

Oftentimes, I have been asked, "What do you get out of the services you give to your church, the schools, and the community in general? You receive no money. What is your reward? How are your compensated?"

Some years ago I noticed in attendance every Sunday at the morning service in my church a very personable woman who had three small children with her. One morning I asked her why the children were not attending Sunday School. Her reply was that there was no one to bring them. The lady was Mrs. Hattie Pitts and one of the children, Janice Lewis, was the child of Mrs. Pitts' daughter Naomi Hardy and Frank and Frances were the twins of another daughter, Mrs. Savage. After much pressure on my part, a way was found. In time, they learned to come alone. Janice learned to play the piano and played for the Sunday School, graduated from the Teachers' College, obtained a teaching position in the local school system. At this time she is married with children whom she brought to the Sunday School that they might receive spiritual training early in their lives. At this writing she is teaching in a Connecticut school system and serving the church there with the same devotion and commitment as she did with her church here in Washington, DC. Frank Savage received his BA degree from Howard University, his Master of Arts degree from the Johns Hopkins School of Advanced International Studies. He served as director of Operation Crossroads Africa and was stationed in the Middle East and Africa from 1964 to 1970. He was a member of the National Small Business Investment Advisory Council and Director of the New York Chapter of the Interracial Council for Business Opportunity. His latest election was as vice president in the bond investment department of the Equitable Life Insurance Society of the US. In 1972 he was selected a member of the *Outstanding Young Men of America*.

Frances Savage, now Mrs. Cherry, is a graduate of Howard University in Social Studies and received a masters degree in business administration from Pace University. In 1970 she joined the Philip Morris Company as Community Relations Coordinator and was named Equal Employment Opportunity Coordinator for Philip Morris Incorporated. She is responsible for coordinating and maintaining the inventory levels of all material used by the field sales force.
Frances is a member of several professional and community organizations, including the Educational Manpower Committee for the United States Chamber of Commerce, the Black Executive Exchange Program of the National Urban League and the Council of Concerned Black Executives. She has been a guest lecturer at Hunter College, and for the

American Management Association and the Milwaukee Businessmen's Association .

I met another of Mrs. Pitts' daughters, Hazel Sands, whose son Teddy is doing well in his chosen field. Everybody loves Hazel because Hazel has so much love for everybody. I love her all the more because of the devoted care she gave her mother during her last days on this earth.

For several Sunday mornings in our Sunday School I noticed an 11 year old girl who was wearing overshoes, although the weather was dry and pleasant. I asked her quietly if she was in need of shoes and she said, "Yes." I talked to the president of one of the church organizations, who said that she had some of her shoes that she would give this little girl. I was so offended that I visited Mrs. Fisher, the president of another organization of the church. Mrs. Fisher promised me that new shoes would be provided. I remember how happy the girl was when she received the shoes. When the Sunday School was asked by the radio station WINX to furnish the program on a Sunday afternoon, this girl took a prominent part. After graduation from high school, she went away to college, where she graduated with honors. She has a good job, is married and worships and works with her husband in another church.

One Sunday a member of my Young People's Sunday School class asked for a conference with me.

Immediately after the close of the class session we found a quiet place, where he confided to me that he was contemplating suicide. I did not panic, but, deep within me, I prayed to God to help me to say something that would avert this young man from carrying out his threat. I said to him, "It appears to me that you're healthy; you have on a nice suit, a nice shirt a nice tie. Are you out of work?" I was saying all this to him while asking God to help me to use the effective words.

"No," he said.

"But why?" I repeated.

He did not tell me why and I did not press for an answer, but I did find words that helped him to think clearly again and I urged him to place himself and that which was torturing him into God's keeping and that God would not fail to sustain him. We talked a long time, and when we parted, I knew that he had abandoned all thought of ending his life. I have always known that teaching in the Sunday School to be a serious calling, but this young man's plight and his confiding in me all the more made me realize the teacher's momentous spiritual responsibility, not only to members of the class, but to the entire school, church, and community. When I was a minister's wife, members of the church unburdened themselves to me when they would not do so to the minister, and I have many confidences locked in a corner of my heart that I have divulged to no one because I deem these confidences a sacred trust.

A young woman called me one night from Philadelphia and said that her name was Malvina. She wanted to know if I remembered her. I told her that I did. "Mrs. Tucker," she said, "*I have made it.* When things went against me in the home where I was a board child, whenever I was around you, you always *took up for me*. That has been quite a few years ago, but I have never forgotten you. I am a teacher in the schools of this city, and I am calling to thank you for having had faith in me and for urging me always to do my best under all circumstances."

When I needed extra help in my office, I would call a Miss Johnson at the Cardozo High School, who would send the type of student I needed. When my work warranted it, I would ask for two or more students. The ones sent to me were from the graduating class. This was part-time work and the students spent the last period of the day with me, for which they were given credit, as if still in the classroom. After graduation they sought full-time employment and I would write letters of recommendation. One student obtained work in a businessman's office near my office. In a few days she came back to me, saying that her employer's attitude was so brusque that she had to tell him that when she and another student came to my office for employment, that, in spite of the fact that the two had to be broken in, Mrs. Tucker never raised her voice at us. She confided in me that while she had to be on the defensive to the extent that she could not work there. At her request, I gave her work and helped her to obtain a full-time job in the government service.

My last surviving sister-in-law, Effie Corrothers-Artis, wrote me from Michigan that there was a young girl in South Bend, Indiana, who wanted to be a singer. Could I get her a job so that she might earn sufficient money to pay her tuition through the music school at Howard University. Berthea and I agreed to invite her to our home. She was, as Effie had said, very much in the Marian Anderson type, only much smaller in physique. I had been told that she could type, so I asked my secretary, Virginia Harris, to test her, and we found that she needed more practice than she was having during intervals at my office, whereupon I rented a typewriter and had it sent to my home. When she made sufficient progress, I helped her with the type of questions she could expect on the test she would have to take. When examined, she failed the first time, the second, and the third time, and she said that she would not try again. Emphatically I said to her, "You are going to continue to take the examination until you pass it and I am going to continue to assist you." On her fourth try she passed the test.

I then took her to her senator's office and soon she received a well-paying job. Later, I went with her to Howard University where Dean Warner Lawson gave her a voice test. In the meantime, I had her placed in the junior choir as well as the senior choir of my church, and when she was called upon to sing on special occasions, I taught her the songs and I accompanied her on the piano. To help her and witness her success was much joy for me.

Many students in the church, and in my neighborhood used my name as a reference on their application forms and as a result FBI agents were constantly visiting my home and at my office to check on the applicants. It was a routine procedure that I had become used to. One day an agent came to my office, where two of my secretaries and I were quietly working. He flamboyantly flashed his credentials on my desk, evidently expecting me to become alarmed. My girls did not raise their eyes from their work and I said, "Well?" He was so bewildered that he knew not how to proceed. When he recovered his composure he stated his mission.

One day when I called Miss Johnson for help she sent me a male student. When he came, I said to him that I wanted a girl, not a boy, whereupon one of the Brotherhood men said, "Now, Sister Tucker, you know you are going to like him and his work." After graduation, he was called to the Armed Services and when he served his time and returned to Washington, he visited me at my office.

On January 7, 1972, one of my former student helpers, Betty Wood, now Mrs. Betty Marshall, called me from Reston, Virginia, telling me that she had often thought of me and decided to talk to me that very day. Two days later, I received a letter from her, stating in part that she was happy that she had called me and that it was nice hearing my voice again after so many years. "Would you believe it has been 21 years since I worked in your office. I have a daughter 18 years old and another daughter seven and a son nine years old. My husband and I both are doing well and our children are healthy and happy." Enclosed were pictures of her three children.

I am tearful as I write this last paragraph, in as much as I have been permitted to touch the lives of so many people, especially young people, through the years. I loved them and enjoyed working with them, and, from time to time, so to speak, many of them have returned to thank me, but, more importantly, I thank them for enriching my life and making it more fruitful and abundant. This is my compensation for which no amount of money could repay.

Appendix II—Four Generations

When Dr. Corrothers and I lived in Philadelphia area we met many people who became our very dear friends. In those days, we found Philadelphia truly to be the "City of Brotherly Love." Most of those I first knew have now passed on. However, there was a family whose friendship developed almost to the level of blood relationship—the family of James H. Saunders, including his wife Jennie, their daughters Helen and Alice, and four sons. When Dr. Corrothers was called to the pastorate of the Second Presbyterian Church of West Chester, our families continued to keep in close touch with each other. Helen married a man by the name of Waddy and while still young, she died, leaving a baby girl, Flora, and an infant son, George. These children the elder Saunders raised as their own. When I first saw Flora, she snuggled into my arms and my heart and there she still remains to this day, after more than 60 years. Flora called her grandmother, Mrs. Saunders, "Mother," and she called me "Aunt," as if the two of us were sisters. Flora, now Mrs. Baker, has four children—two girls and two boys. Mr. Baker, the husband, has been dead about four years. So, you see I have been intimately associated with four generations of the Saunders family: Mrs. Jennie Saunders, her daughter Helen and her granddaughter, Flora Baker, and her great granddaughter Flora, named after her mother. I must say that Alice and her niece Flora try their best to fill in for my loss of Mrs. Saunders, who died several years ago. Alice remembers me on my every birthday, on Mother's Day, and on Christmas, with a gift or a check. Whenever Flora hears that I am ill, she will leave everything and rush from Philadelphia to Washington to see Aunt Rosina. When I was sick in the hospital four years ago, one Sunday morning I awoke, and there, standing by my bed was Flora, who had gotten word through a mutual friend that I was ill. She had arrived at the station on Saturday night on time, but she had to wait three hours for a cab because of a heavy snow storm. She remained with me all that Sunday; she returned Monday morning to be with me until train time that afternoon. Such concern and devotion shown to me by this and previous and subsequent deeds are treasures that no amount of money can buy. The Saunders family of Philadelphia is the first family I have known and with whom I have been closely associated through four generation.

For years it was the custom of the Fifteenth Street Presbyterian Church to invite all visitors and strangers in attendance to register their names and addresses in a book placed for that purpose in the vestibule of the edifice. A committee known as the "Strangers Committee" would then see that those registered were visited. In time I came to be the "visitor" of that committee. Because of my position, I became acquainted with many people, among whom were the McCottry family: Mr. Samuel McCottry, his wife Anna, and the two very small daughters, Gwendolyn and Miriam, and the still smaller boys, Samuel, Jr. and James. Another son, Wilbur, came along a few years later. When Gwen and Miriam grew older, they would walk to my home each Sunday morning and I would take them to Sunday School. This continued until they learned the way and could go alone. Each girl took lessons on the piano from me and when I organized the "Northeast Players", a group of high school girls and boys, they were instrumental in helping me select the type of talent I needed in the near Northeast area. My most beautiful play, "The Queen of the Roses," which I staged, was composed of recitations, dialogues, solos, and choruses all about roses. The finale was a series of beautiful calisthenics. Our first performance was at the Fifteenth Street Presbyterian Church, where it was received enthusiastically. We were invited to perform at other churches and to repeat the play several times. Finally, we had to refuse because my players were still in school.

So, my second family of four generations is the McCottry family, whose careers I have observed and helped to develop to a small degree. Brother Samuel B. McCottry and my second husband Brother B.J. Tucker were in the

Pullman service. When the Brotherhood of Sleeping-Car Porters was organized, both of these men became charter members, and when I organized the wives, Sister McCottry became a charter member of the Ladies Auxiliary. Their family had vital interests in two fields: religion and labor. Gwendolyn married Ralph Branson Miller, who was one of the students who had a part in my plays. Gwen has one daughter, who is Mrs. Murphy, and she, in turn, has a daughter Leslie. We have the four generations here: Mrs. Anna McCottry, her daughter Gwendolyn Miller, granddaughter Barbara Miller Murphy, and great-granddaughter Leslie Murphy. Gwendolyn McCottry Miller became a communicant member of the Fifteenth Street Presbyterian Church at the age of 14 and is an important member of several organizations of the church and she is active in many areas of church fellowship. She is a graduate and post-graduate of Cardozo Business High School, a graduate of the St. Paul Institute of Nursing; is the past president of the Business and Professional Women's Club; past secretary of the Police Boys Club and retired Secretary of the Army Material Command. She has been especially been interested in her community's schools, having served as president of the Parent Teacher Association. She is sensitive to the personal needs of indigents wherever they may be.

Miriam McCottry, the second daughter, now Mrs. Andrew Bell, graduated from Dunbar High School and then the Howard University College of Dentistry, specializing in Dental Hygiene, then a new course, this being the second year of its existence. She was graduated, passed the Board of Examiners, but, because of her race, could not obtain an appointment in the Government Treasury Department. In the meantime, since she has always liked to work with her hands, she entered the Roosevelt Night High School for a course in Home Catering, specializing in cake baking and decorating. During this time she was transferred from the Treasury Department to the Health, Education, and Welfare Department. During this period, she took a course in enameling on copper, making earrings, bracelets, cufflinks, and necklaces. She took this course as a hobby, but the accruement from her sales was rather substantial indeed. She is now with the D.C. Public Department of Pupil Personnel as a liaison teacher between the student, parent, and the home. This position demands a sensitivity to the personal needs of the student, such as food, direction where to go for shoes and clothing, and making appointments for medical and dental treatment. This job demands expertise and a sympathetic approach, and Miriam has both in abundance. She has four children: three girls and a boy. The oldest girl is an artist, her second girl is a clothes designer, the youngest girl is still in school, and her son, the oldest, among other of his talents, is a gourmet chef.

Samuel B. McCottry the oldest son of the family, after graduating from the public schools, entered the Howard University School of Medicine in Washington, D.C., and was graduated with a B.S. and M.D. degree. He served in active combat during World War II, leaving military service as a Captain of Infantry. After post-graduate training at Freedmen's Hospital in Washington, he entered private practice in Internal Medicine and began service as University Physician at the University Health Service at Howard University in 1953, progressing to Associate Director, and in 1967, Director, which position he still holds. He is at present a member of the D.C. Metropolitan Interagency at American University; he has participated in the National Coordinating Council on Drug Education. Dr. McCottry was the co-sponsor of a Seminar Series on Human Sexuality, which was instituted at Howard University. Here he instituted a counseling program for Sickle Cell Disease and is a panelist for the Review of Drug Education Broadcast Material for the American Science Film Association. He is known as a family doctor. He has been a trustee in the Fifteenth Street Presbyterian Church and is now and has been for several years an Elder, and has chaired many important committees. His wife Mildred is a product of the Washington public schools. She has a B.A. degree in English and German and a M.A. degree in English literature. She has taught in the D.C. Public Schools and at Howard University. She is active in the work of the church and the community and at present is the president of the Women's Organization of the church.

The second son, James McDowell McCottry, was graduated from Armstrong Technical High School in Washington and then entered the Industrial School at Savannah, Georgia, where he pursued a business course and studied shoemaking. His ambition was not only to make shoes but to design them, specializing in orthopedic shoemaking. In fact, he wanted to make all types of leather articles, such as hand-bags, pocketbooks, and other things in the same line. His dream was to learn all that he could in leather artistry so as to open a shop equipped principally with his own handiwork. At this time his father became ill and James was unable to remain in school, and so he came back to Washington, DC, took the Civil Service Examination and was appointed to the U.S. Accounting Office, and afterwards took a position in the U.S. Postal Service, from which he retired in 1977. He transacts much of the family's business and is now chairman of the Trustee Board of the Fifteenth Street Presbyterian Church, which office is a responsibility, as the church is now in the process of rebuilding. His wife Lorraine, after graduation from Dunbar

High School, obtained a position in the State Department Intelligence and Research Division. When she retired she was the Administrative Assistant to a city council member. James and Lorraine McCottry are the parents of two sons and a two week old granddaughter at this writing.

Wilbur McCottry, the youngest of the children, was graduated from Spingarn High School and enlisted in the Navy, where he went to school and was graduated from dental technology and radiology schools. He served three years, all told, in the Navy. He is now employed by the U.S. Army at Walter Reed Army Hospital as Chief Dental Radiology Technician. His wife Jeanette graduated from Dunbar High School and the D.C. Teachers' College with a B.S. in elementary education and is a teacher in the D.C. Public School systems. Wilbur and Jeanette are the parents of two sons.

To have observed, step by step, the development of these families through four generations warrants special mention.

Appendix III-Testimonial Dinner, Public Interest Civic Association

The Public Interest Civic Association gave me a dinner in my honor on my retirement as [its] president on Tuesday, September 10, 1957, at 8:00 PM at the YWCA Annex, 1719 13th Street, N.W., at which time more than fifty representatives [were present] from various church, civic, educational, and labor [organizations] gathered for the occasion. Dr. Jesse A. Keen, acting president, presided. Mrs. Columbia Scott, first vice-president, was Mistress of Ceremony. Expressions of appreciation were tendered by the Rev. Dr. Robert P. Johnson, Pastor of the Fifteenth Street Presbyterian Church; the Rev. Dr. J.L.S. Holloman, pastor of the Second Baptist Church, and the Rev. J.D. Foy, pastor of the Asbury Methodist Church. Representing organized labor were Mr. Theodore Brown, International Director of Research and Education of the BSCP, New York City; Mrs. Elizabeth Craig, President of the local Ladies Auxiliary; and Mr. W.S. Calloway of the local Brotherhood. Representing the Federation of Civic Associations were Attorney Barrington Parker, president, and pastor presidents Mr. Woolsey Hall and Dr. Herbert C. Marshall. Also, there were Mrs. Alpha Jones of the Board of Public Welfare and Mr.

Robert Brooks, president of the Parent Teachers Association Congress. Mrs. Jones and Mr. Brooks had been closely associated with me in this, the near Northeast area for many years. The principal speaker, Dr. E.F. Harris, past president of the Federation reminded those present that the Public Interest Civic Association had not functioned for many years and when Mrs. Tucker took over it became one of the strongest associations of the Federation. He said that Mrs. Tucker's dedication as chairman of the Social Service Committee and her outstanding achievement of her program attracted the attention and admiration of the membership, so that in a short time she was voted the first vice-president of the Federation. Up to that time there had been only two other women vice-presidents: Mrs. Corinne Martin and Mrs. Velma Williams. Dr. Harris added, "How splendid it would be if we had more and more Rosina Tuckers!"

The consensus of the speeches was: Mrs. Tucker has worked with diligence, courage of conviction and unswerving strength and devotion. Her service includes three fields: Labor, Social Service, and Religion. She has worked to achieve betterment in the school problem areas; spearheaded a drive to get an additional wing built on the Logan School at 3rd and G Streets, N.E.;
Served on the Board of Commissions Committee of Juvenile Delinquency in Area "P"; has served as First Vice-President

for two terms in the Federation of Civic Associations and as chairman of its Social Service Committee, the scope of which includes all the institutions under the Board of Public Welfare.

She has testified before Senate and House committees relative to District suffrage and schools and day care centers; has lobbied on Capitol Hill for labor, schools, and district affairs; and has worked closely with the United Community Services. In 1955, she received the NAACP Silver Cup for outstanding service through the years. For 32 years she has been one of the pillars in the organization of the Brotherhood of Sleeping-Car Porters and has served as International Secretary-Treasurer of its Ladies Auxiliary for 18 years to date. She is a member of the Fifteenth Street Presbyterian Church; a teacher of its young adult class of church school, comprised of Howard University and Miner Teachers College students; is an Elder, the first woman officer in the history of the church, and the president of the Trustee Board.

Those who have worked with and closely associated with Mrs. Tucker express regret that such a fine leader is leaving.

Every year the Federation of Civic Associations recognizes the outstanding work of its members by honoring them at the annual Awards Banquet. According, when it is desired that a member of the District of Columbia Federation of Civic Associations be honored, the member association makes the request. This is that statement sent from the Public Interest Civic Association to the Federation of Civic Associations, written by the corresponding secretary, Mr. George D. Brown:

As a committee representing the Public Interest Civic Association, we solicit your attention to meritorious civic activity as exemplified by Mrs. Rosina Corrothers Tucker, in your consideration of the award represented by the D.C. NAACP Trophy. The scope of Mrs. Tucker's work has exceeded the boundaries of the local area of the Public Interest Civic Association; it has been made manifest throughout the entire community of civic associations in the District of Columbia and, indeed, nationally in its implications.

Mrs. Tucker served 12 years as president of the Northeast Women's Club, whose two main projects are the sending of boys and girls to camp and the giving of cash prizes to graduates of the Vocational School. She is serving her 15 year as president of the Public Interest Civic Association; she served for two terms as vice president of the Federation of Civic Associations and was a member of the advisory committee of the OPA during World War II. In 1940 she was selected by the U.S. Labor Department to represent Labor in an exhibit at the Chicago Exposition, depicting 75 years of progress of American Negro women in the Labor field.

In 1945, when the plebiscite was held relative to suffrage in the District, Mrs. Tucker was given charge of two polling districts. She was the only woman of her race on a committee of 24 to investigate the Community Chest of Greater Washington in 1947, in which assignment she helped to write a minority report. The majority report excludes such agencies as the YMCA and YWCA, both black and white, and the Urban League. As a result of the minority report, the Chest was reorganized and these agencies were retained. She was also the only black woman on a committee that worked for three years making a survey of the Children's Services under the Board of Public Welfare; was requested by the full committee to write the reports on the National Training School for Girls and the Industrial Home for Boys. Her report, together with the other reports on the institutions were studied, assimilated, and put in book form by the United Community Services. The book is used for social study by church, social, and labor groups—about sixteen other groups in all.

The unique service which Mrs. Tucker rendered to the Children's Services was well described by Mr. Paul Cherney, Secretary, United Community Services, on the occasion of a testimonial banquet in her honor on October 30, 1954. Mr. Cherney stated that on the meeting of the committee in 1950, the chart which they found had been promulgated fourteen years before and at the rate of prior accomplishment by the record, the prospect was that the plans would be about 30 years in achievement. On the tenacious insistence of Mrs. Tucker, conditions in the institutions were publicized by photographs and articles in the Evening Star. Instead of a 30 years lag, the plans were completed in this year 1955, the buildings having been dedicated in September.

Dr. C. Herbert Marshall emphasized on the same occasion that it is of utmost significance that the services rendered by Mrs. Tucker were for all the children, not for the black community, not for the black children, but for all the children.

When the girls of the National Training School were to be transferred to the Industrial Home for Boys at Blue Plains, Mrs. Tucker took it upon herself to inspect the two buildings to be occupied by these girls and approved the change and so recommended it to the Federation.

Mrs. Tucker has testified before Senate and House committees relative to labor, District suffrage, schools, and day care centers. She has testified before the Commissioners, the Board of Education, and Recreation

Board relative to more and better school buildings and more adequate and non-segregated recreational facilities.

She has served as a member of the East Capitol Area Citizen's Youth Project, Area "P" of the Commissioners' Youth Council, studying Juvenile Delinquency; she is an elder of the Fifteenth Street Presbyterian Church; she is the president of its Trustee Board and a teacher of the young people's church school class. She was the first woman officer in the history of the church.

We, as a committee, submit that out of the many and varied public-spirited contributions of Mrs. Tucker, both vital and unique in character, it is entirely proper that she should receive special recognition. Respectfully submitted

George D. Brown, Chairman

Columbia Scott, 2nd vice-president

Agnes Coleman, Secretary

Public Interest Civic Association

The Federation committee on awards deliberations acceded to the Public Interest's request and at the Annual Federation of Civic Association's Awards Banquet, held in the ballroom of Mayflower Hotel, December 7, 1955, Attorney Eugene Davidson, President of the DC Branch of the NAACP, after a very appropriate speech, presented me the NAACP Silver Cup, the highest award given by the Federation. My reply follows:

Mr. President, officers, members and friends, may I take this opportunity to thank the Committee on Awards for citing me for the NAACP trophy, and may I thank Mr. Davidson for his splendid presentation speech. I have known Mr. Davidson for some time; also I knew his father, having worked with him during the time he was an important official of the NAACP. That was a number of years ago and when I was a very young woman.

About 10 years ago, Dr. Harris, the president of this body, appointed me to serve as the chairman of the Social Service Committee, at which time I knew not the ramifications of this particular committee, but I soon learned that all the institutions under the Board of Public Welfare and a few others were included in its scope. Mr. Mr. Woolsey Hall became president, to me it seemed that every phase of the Federation's work was under my committee. Anywhere from 4 to 6 o'clock AM or at midnight, he would call requesting me to testify at certain Senate, House, or District hearings, often scheduled for 10 o'clock in the morning. I did not fare quite so badly under the succeeding presidents.

My committee could not cover in detail all of the services, as special attention was given to the National Training School for Girls and the Industrial Home for Boys. One day I met on the street one of the delegates from this body who asked, "Mrs. Tucker, how are your girls getting along?" I was puzzled. I knew I had reared two boys, but no girls. Seeing my confusion, he said, "I mean your girls at the Training School." Well, I considered this a compliment, for I was happy to be identified with this group of girls and to serve in the area where the need was so pressing.

When I visited the School for the feeble minded, I was deeply impressed with the unfortunate children there-in. No matter how extensive their affliction, I was sensitive to their desire for love and understanding, for so many of them would meet me with outstretched arms, inviting me to take them into mine—these were white children. Not only at this particular school does this obtain, but at other institutions, it was only necessary to look into the eyes of these disturbed children to see the conflict in their souls.

At Junior Village, there are children who are orphans, others have been abandoned, many of whom from birth have known no other home but that institution. At this Christmas season, can't you invite one or two of these children to spend the Christmas season, or at least spend Christmas day in your home? It is known that some people have enjoyed having two or more of these children with them for as long as two weeks.

You represent the entire citizenry of the District and I am hopeful that many of you younger members will dedicate yourselves to the entire program of the Federation, thereby assuming your portion of its enormous responsibilities to the community—its spiritual responsibility, civil, social, educational, and legal.

There is a verse of Scripture that has intrigued me for a number of years. It is: "Whosoever will save his life shall lose it, but whosoever will lose his life for my sake, the same shall save it." A paradox, you say? Truly, for it is hard to understand; nevertheless it is true, for only those who actually lose themselves serving others can understand this seeming contradiction. Only those who serve selflessly can attain the plateau of saving his own life.

Again, I humbly thank the Committee for its citation. I thank the Federation for approving the award, and I thank the NAACP for providing the Award. I thank you.

The banquet was a brilliant affair. The principal speaker was Dr. Lester B. Granger, Executive Director of the Urban League.

Of great importance to the occasion is the presentation of the Federation's annual awards to the association having done the most outstanding job and the individual having done an exceptional civic job. The association receiving the trophy contributed by the *Evening Star* newspaper was Mrs. Ella R. Foster, President of the Douglas Heights Association, and I, the president of the Public Interest Association received the NAACP trophy for the individual having done an exceptional civic job.

Rev. Robert Pierre Johnson, my pastor, and a platform guest, placed the following statement in the bulletin of church announcements: *"Our own Mrs. Rosina C. Tucker and Mr. Woolsey W. Hall figured prominently at the Twenty-Fifth Annual Dinner of the Federation of Civic Associations last Wednesday at the Mayflower Hotel. Mrs. Tucker received the highest award, the NAACP Loving Cup Award for notable public service and Mr. Woolsey Hall presented the Federation Citation to Dr. Walter E. Hager, President of the District of Columbia Teachers' College. We are proud of these loyal members of our church who are also distinguished civic leaders of the District."*

Appendix IV—A Scroll

I was honored with a testimonial banquet November 18, 1966 by the Brotherhood of Sleeping-Car Porters at the Presidential Arms Hotel. On a page beside my picture in the souvenir program folder was the following statement:

A native of Washington, DC, at 83 [sic]—the youngest among us. She is one of the most motivated public spirited citizens of the District. Mrs. Tucker is an accomplished musician, playing the organ, piano, and violin. In addition, she has written scores of music and at 14 was the organist for one of the largest churches in the District.

In 1925, when the Brotherhood was organized, Pullman porters throughout the nation were victims of Pullman propaganda. Many lost jobs and the fear of "Pullman" manifested itself in most of the homes of the porters. In order to stop the flight of the porters from the Brotherhood, Mrs. Tucker became the organizer of the division and assisted in organizing the International Ladies' Auxiliary. She was the first president of the Washington Division Ladies Auxiliary and the first secretary-treasurer of the International Ladies' Auxiliary. She has made a lasting contribution to every major project sponsored by the Brotherhood, including the original "March on Washington" movement in 1942 that secured the first FEPC.

Mrs. Tucker served 12 years as the president of the Northeast Women's Club. She had an exhibit at the Chicago Exposition depicting "Seventy-five Years of Progress of the American Negro Woman." She represented the Brotherhood and its Auxiliary at many important labor conferences over the years. Her talents have been used widely by the community, having been called upon to testify before House and Senate committees on District suffrage. She also testified before the Board of Education and lobbied for the teachers' union.

Mrs. Tucker is a member of the East Capitol Area Citizens' Youth Project, Area "P" of the Commissioners' Youth Council, a member of the Fifteenth Street Presbyterian Church, and vice-president of its trustee board.

She has won our love, respect, and admiration for her loyalty, devotion, and dedication to the Brotherhood and the organized labor movement.

On the scroll was this statement:

Brotherhood of Sleeping-Car Porters, an international union, affiliated with the AFL—CIO, this woman is known and judged by the record she makes which her fellow sisters appraise and keep. Daily, this woman sets down for the study and judgment of her fellow sisters in words and deeds, the core of her character. Our contemporary co-workers and friends applaud and condemn us for what we do and say in the fleeting moments that pass. Whether the community in which we live is better because we have passed this way on our journey from the cradle to the grave is a challenge and choice which each of us must meet and make from day to day. Because of your vital decision in the yesteryears to throw your lot with your fellow workers and sisters, banded together in the Brotherhood of Sleeping-Car Porters and Ladies' Auxiliary for the purpose of working and fighting for decent standards of living and a happier tomorrow; because you, in the face of opposition, trials, and tribulations, remained steadfast and immoveable in your devotion and loyalty to the Brotherhood and Ladies' Auxiliary; and since, in the judgment of the officers and members of our Great Movement, you have fought the good fight and kept the faith as a good Auxiliary member, the organization has elected, in appreciation of your contribution to the building of a bigger and better Brotherhood and Ladies' Auxiliary, and as a token of your courage, vision, and integrity in remaining a faithful member, to give you, MRS. ROSINA TUCKER, this award, in the form of this Scroll of Honor. May you keep and cherish it all the days of your life and hand it down as a priceless heritage to those of your kith and kin and coming *generations for their inspiration and faith in the long, hard, and bitter struggles of the Sleeping-Car Porters, Chair Car Attendants and Train Porters and Ladies' Auxiliaries in building for themselves in particular and the workers of all races, colors, religions, and national origins in general, a trade union of freedom, plenty, justice, and equality.*

Peace be unto you! May Heaven bless and keep you! Brotherhood of Sleeping-Car Porters.

[signed]
A. Philip Randolph
Benjamin F. McLaurin

Appendix V–Dr. Robert Pierre Johnson's Severance Speech

One Sunday in August, 1967, during the social hour which occurs immediately after the morning service, coming out of a special committee meeting, an officer informed me that I had been selected to represent the church at Presbytery and to make the severance speech on the occasion of Dr. Robert Pierre Johnson's departure from Washington to become the Moderator of the New York City Presbytery. I was rather surprised, because, several years before, I had the same assignment when our pastor, Dr. Halley B. Taylor, resigned the pastorate of the church. I began my speech by delineating Dr. Johnson's varied accomplishments before coming to Washington and his church-wide and community-wide accomplishments during his tenure here. Then I continued:

When my former husband, Rev. Dr. James David Corrothers was a young struggling writer, he received a letter from the well-known Ella Wheeler Wilcox,[104] a writer of books, a contributor to magazines and periodicals, who also wrote syndicated columns which were carried in newspapers throughout the United States. One sentence in

---

[104] Ella Wheeler Wilcox (1850-1919) was a writer of popular poetry.

the letter she wrote was "Enter every open door." Therefore, I considered this assignment an open door for me to enter with the hope that I might in some way sensitize your thinking and action in the new phase of our history. Therefore, kindly permit to read two poems, each by that struggling writer I mentioned above and, while written over 50 years ago, you can see their poignancy today. The first one, "Driftwood" is in Negro dialect, the second, "At the Closed Gate of Justice," is in literary English.

Driftwood

The driftwood drifts down the river with the tide
Or lodges on the bank along the river side,
But the steamboat splutters and splashes up the stream,
A-puffing and a-pounding and a-blowing of her steam.
The white folk is like steamboats, steering where they please
Along Life's happy river, in their swiftness and pride,
But the Negro is more often like the driftwood he sees
A-floating, floating, floating with the tide.
Just sit down there by the bayou or the stream
And philosophize awhile where the driftwood dream.
All weather-beat and water-logged, idle there it lay—
Frogs and owls for company, through the nights and days,
But you can't no way fault it! T'were the tide or gale
Left it in the lily-ponds, 'long the river side—
Neath the moon a-dreaming where the willows trail—

Just a–waiting, waiting, waiting for the tide.

The steamboat sure is a mighty pretty sight,
A-making for a point 'way yonder, day or night.
And what's the driftwood bobbing round and bumping 'neath her keel,
Unless it whirl up through the foam and clog her paddle-wheel?
But that don't pestacate her long 'fore off she puts some more,
A-tearing up the river, belching resin, fat, and pine!
But when you see a Negro stand and watch her from the shore
Just think about the driftwood, whirling there behind!

It's work, then it's loaf, dabble here and drabble there—
It's sneers to swallow down, and it's heap o'pain to bear;
It's courting and it's dancing, hope, religion jubilee—
It's whiskey and the devil and the penitentiary!
Oh, it's wife and little children, unprotected, scattered 'round—
Just black and helpless driftwood sticking here and sinking there,
A-mingling and a-marrying with other driftwood, bound
From nowhere down to no place, toting nothing but despair.

The song and the dance and the plunking of the tune
Ends in the dark at the setting of the moon,
Just like the hopes of the black-faced race—

> *Why it's hoot owl and whip-po-will, but, Negro, know your place!*
> *We're free, but free like driftwood in the wet and cold,*
> *Fit for frogs and turtles, or for fuel!—till we're gone;*
> *The saddest sight I know of is a Negro, growing old,*
> *Drifting towards the willows, drifting on and on.*

At the Closed Gate of Justice

by James David Corrothers

To be a Negro in a day like this
Demands forgiveness. Bruised with blow on blow,
Betrayed, like him whose woe-dimmed eyes gave bliss,
Still must one succor those who brought one low
To be a Negro in a day like this.

To be a Negro in a day like this
Demands a rare patience----patience that can wait
In utter darkness. 'T is the path to miss,
And knock, unheeded, at an iron gate,
To be a Negro in a day like this.

To be a Negro in a day like this
Demands strange loyalty. We serve a flag
Which is to us white freedom's emphasis,
Ah! One must love when truth and justice lag
To be a Negro in a day like this.

To be a Negro in a day like this—
Alas! Lord God, what evil have we done?
Still shines the gate, all gold and amethyst,

"Mere a Negro"—in a day like this.

In the "Driftwood" poem you have a work picture of a filthy slum wherein the dwellers
had little hope of escape—all doors were closed. There was desperation, suffering, hopelessness, and a sense of abandonment, but no resentment or inclination to retaliate.

In the second poem, "At the Closed Gate of Justice", in some mysterious way a Negro here and there crawled out of this mud and muck, worked, studied, sacrificed, hoped and prayed for better things to find that no only were doors closed, but an iron gate erected against his ambitions. These two poems were written over 50 years ago; they applied then, they applied over 100 years ago. They no longer apply today, for there is now deep resentment and a noticeable feeling of retaliation born of a growing loss of faith. There is no a growing distrust of the white man. I am proud of the knowledge that at the close of the Civil War, white northern women went to the south to teach ex-slaves and their children to read and write, and, really, Johnny learned to read and write in those days. I am proud of those women also because they suffered ostracism and unmentionable humiliation, but that they formed the nucleus of the Presbyterian Church in the South—in such places as Virginia and North and South Carolina, where sincerity and *dignity of workmanship was established. I am proud that the offspring of those Negroes who migrated to the North helped to organize colored Presbyterian churches in many northern cities, such as Washington, Philadelphia, New York, Baltimore, Chicago, St. Louis, etc. I am proud of the churches, the schools and hospitals you have built. You have succored Negro Presbyterians in their efforts for advancement in areas of education, in the field of civil rights. You have rallied with us; you have sung with us; you have been reviled and spat upon with us and some have died with us. For this I and my people are grateful to you.*

But we cannot stop at this point, for there is much more soul-searching to be made. We must listen to the cries of anguish of Negro men and women, boys and girls who are striving for education, jobs, and job security and the benefits of the American society. These Negroes are not lazy—they want jobs. They are not radicals, but are devoid of that hope that should come with youth, and instead, there is bitterness. Bitterness, anger and frustration are the birthright of the Negro. They are not extremists or haters, but are at the end of their rope.

Friends, I must confess that my address is not conventional for this occasion, but I had to enter this open door to tell you some of the serious thoughts that trouble the hearts and lives of my people.

You know, of course, the Bible story of Esther, a member of the then-hated Jewish race, and how she pleaded with the king to deliver her and her people from the hostile schemes of Haman—so do I, a member of the hated Negro race, plead with you, the leaders of the local Presbyterian Church, whose influence reaches throughout the entire United States, that you resurrect your pioneering spirit and make a study of Negro history from Africa to the present day and see that it is taught in your schools, seminaries, and colleges, and that results of each study appear in your church periodicals. I plead with you to tell your people that Negroes worked on the farms and in the cotton fields of the South for hundreds of years without compensation; that the South became rich on free labor, and, in turn, the cotton, wool, and other materials were transported to the North where the textile manufacturers became rich.

I plead with you to let it be known that there are artists among my people—such as painters, sculptors, musicians who have written symphonies; coloratura sopranos, noted contraltos, tenors, and bassos. I pled that it be made known that we have Negro manufacturers and men who have designed certain safety devices for trains and other vehicles. That we have been of letters in our race: poets, journalists, editors and editorial writers, newspapermen, attorneys and judges, college professors, philosophers, scientists, and specialists in all fields of medicine. There are many other contributions Negroes have given to this, their country.

One fact I must emphasize is that Negroes are not immigrants—they did not leave Africa because of oppression, but they were brought over against their will, and here they shall remain. The whole fuss and furor in this country made by Negroes and other minority groups is that they are under-represented among the best kinds of employment; under-represented in better schools; under-represented among those receiving quality medical care and over-represented among the unemployed. Our society makes room for one Negro now and then, but our system must make room for every Negro.

Friends, what our country needs to understand is that it is poisoned to its soul by racism, and that heroic methods have to be used to save our nation and that each one of you must dedicate yourself an apostle to teach the masses that there must not be two United States of Americas—one white and one black, but that we are all citizens and doors must be opened to all; that all iron gates must be demolished and that all my enter into the highest echelon according to our ability.

God bless you, Mr. Moderator. God bless all you fathers, God bless you brothers and God go with you and dwell with you, our beloved Reverend Johnson. Thank you.

At the close of my speech I was given a rising ovation, led by the Moderator himself. In a few days later I received a request from the Presbyterian office for a copy of the speech, which was duplicated, and copies were sent to all the churches in the Presbytery.

Index

Alexander, Jeremiah "Ike" 176
Alexander, Marietta Harvey Clinkscales 9, 20, 22, 45, 46-47, 49, 50, 176, 179-180, 182, 183, 219, 220, 237
Baker, Flora Waddy 258, 259
Barrier, Mollie 128
Best, Luke 102
Best, Mary Harvey 8, 102
Bethune, Mary McLeod 146-147, 189
Blake, Eva Harvey 7, 235
Blount, Frederick 4
Blount, Jane 4
Blount, Louis 4, 6
Bonus March (1932) 184-185
Brooks, Walter 41
Brotherhood of Sleeping-Car Porters 130-144, 160-184, 186, 188-189, 202, 204-218, 242, 244, 261, 277-279
Brown, George 176, 177, 178, 179
Brown, George D. 156, 272
Brown, Jeannette Harvey "Nettie" 5, 9, 20, 22, 34, 49, 53, 176-177, 178-179, 245n
Bruce, Blanche K. 38
Burgess, Viola Robinson 181
Capper, Arthur 198
Carson, Simeon 97
Chase, Calvin 40
Chateauvert, Melinda viii
Cheatham, Henry 40
Cherry, Frances Savage, 250-251
Cheyney Training School for Teachers 86
Clinkscales, Marietta, see Alexander, Marietta Harvey Clinkscales
Clinkscales, Marion 46-47, 176
Collier, Hattie 24
Connors, John 95
Cook, John Francis 113

Cooper, Anna Haywood 41
Corrothers, Alford 60n
Corrothers, Edwin 60n
Corrothers, Effie 60n, 67, 74, 255
Corrothers, Fannie Clemens 63
Corrothers, Frances 60n
Corrothers, Harriet 60n
Corrothers, Henry Harvey "Hank" (son of Rosina Tucker) xi, 56n, 59, 64, 79, 81-83, 89, 91, 96, 102, 109, 128, 162-174, 177, 190-191, 192-193, 245n
Corrothers, James David (first husband of Rosina Tucker) 54, 56, 59, 65, 66-67, 68, 70, 71, 75-76, 77, 78, 79-80, 81, 83, 84-85, 86-89, 90, 92-93, 95, 104, 105, 163, 164, 224, 240, 258, 281-285
Corrothers, James R. 60n, 67
Corrothers, Minnie 60n, 74
Corrothers, Norman 60n, 74
Corrothers, Oscar 60n, 74
Corrothers, Richard 63
Corrothers, Sarah 60n
Corrothers, Willard Dumas (step-son of Rosina Tucker) 56n, 63, 64, 79, 81-83, 87, 89, 91, 94, 96, 162-163, 174
Craig, Elizabeth 206
Cummings, Elizabeth 95
Cummings, Wayne 95
Curry, James 95
Dawson, William Levi 197-198
Douglass, Frederick 40
Downingtown Industrial and Agricultural School 86
Drew, Charles R. 29
DuBois, William Edward Burghardt 160, 161
Dunbar, Paul Laurence 52, 63
Dunlap, Coleman 90
Dunlap, Eunice 90n, 91-92
Dunlap, Mahala 90-92, 193, 222
Eastland (ship) 70-71
Ellington, Edward K "Duke" 47

Elms, Arthur 138
Epicureans (social club) 45-46
Europe, James Reese 49
Federation of Civic Associations 156, 197-198, 199, 266, 268
Fifteenth Street Presbyterian Church (Washington, DC) 95-96, 112-114, 116-119, 120-129, 193, 201, 229-230, 245, 248, 250, 252-253, 259-260, 268, 278,
Foraker, Joseph 78
Freedmen's Hospital (Washington, DC) 32, 96-97
Frye, Clifford 95
Ganges, Alice 95n
Ganges, Dorothy 95m
Ganges, George 95
Ganges, Herman 95n
Ganges, Melba 95
Ganges, Roland 95n
Garnet, Henry Highland 113
Grandison, Charles W. 62
Graves, Harry 171
Gregory, Pope 146, 167
Grimke, Francis J. 40, 116-117, 118n, 121-125, 167-168
Hall, Elizabeth Bamfield 39, 118-119, 181
Hall, Woolsey 118, 195-196, 197, 266, 275
Hammond, John 141
Hardy, Naomi 250
Harris, Edward 155-156, 157, 201, 266, 273
Harris, Virginia 150, 255
Harvey, Benjamin Turner 9, 19, 26, 45, 47, 50, 54, 179-180, 182, 245n
Harvey, Bessie 180
Harvey, Corinne 9, 34-35
Harvey, Ethel 178, 245n
Harvey, Eva, see Blake, Eva Harvey
Harvey, Griffin 7, 245n
Harvey, Harry 6-7, 245n
Harvey, Harry Augustus 9, 19-20, 177-178, 245n

Harvey, Henrietta Mills 8-9, 16, 18, 22, 25, 26, 29, 31, 34, 36, 43-44, 45, 53, 64, 80, 94, 96, 179-180, 181, 183, 245n
Harvey, Hugh 178, 245n
Harvey, James Henry 9
Harvey, Jeanette (afterwards Turner) 2, 4, 6, 7-8, 20, 22-23, 245n
Harvey, Jeanette Caroline, see Brown, Jeanette Harvey
Harvey, Katherine 2, 4, 7, 33, 245n
Harvey, Lawrence 7
Harvey, Lee Roy 2, 5, 8, 9-11, 14, 15-16, 17-18, 19, 20-21, 22, 25-26, 28, 29, 31-32, 33, 36, 40, 43-44, 45, 50, 53, 80, 245n
Harvey, Lee Roy Graham 9, 34
Harvey, Maria Macon 6n, 7n
Harvey, Marietta Lela, see Alexander, Marietta Harvey Clinkscales
Harvey, Mary, see Best, Mary Harvey
Harvey, Pearl 178
Harvey, Roberta Ann 9
Harvey, Rosina Budd, see Tucker, Rosina Corrothers
Harvey, Sidney 7
Harvey, Virginia Baylor 7n
Health conditions in 1890s 32-33
House, Bernice Stewart 114n, 117n
Howard Theater (Washington, DC) 108, 110, 115, 147
Hubbard, Louise Jones iii, iv
Hundley, Mary Gibson Brewer 42n
Hunter, Alice 200
Industrial Home for Colored Boys 157, 198-199, 271, 273
Johnson, Anna Ganges 95
Johnson, Ella 211
Johnson, Robert Pierre 118n, 224-225, 266, 275, 281, 289
Johnson, William Bishop 36-37, 75, 113
Jones, George M. 76
Jones, James 167
Junior Village 158, 273-274
Keen, Jesse 156

Knickerbocker Theater (Washington, DC) 177
Ladies Auxiliary, Brotherhood of Sleeping-Car Porters 115, 145-150, 188, 190, 201, 202-204, 206, 218,, 261, 278
LaGuardia, Fiorello 185, 186, 187
Langston, John Mercer 39
Lee, George Wellington 42
Lee, John W. 84, 119-120, 168
Lewis, Janice 250
Lloyd, Henry D. 62
Loving, Walter 19
Lynch, John Roy 39
M Street High School 50-52, 57, 154
Madella, Louise 226
March on Washington (1963) 187-188
Marshall, Betty Wood 257
Marshall, Herbert, Sr. 170-171
McCottry Family 260-265
McDaniel, Norma 243, 244
McKinley, William 66
McLaurin, Benjamin F. iv, v, x, 182-183, 205, 277-279
McMillan, Beatrice 194
Meyer, Agnes 199
Mills, Henrietta, see Harvey, Henrietta Mills
Miner, James 76
Mount Olive Baptist Church 80, 160
Mount Olivet Receiving Home 199
Murray, Loree vi, xi
NAACP 160-161, 187, 268
National Training School for Colored Girls 157, 198-199, 271, 273
Nixon, Edgar Daniel 209-211
Nixon, Richard M. 230-232
Northeast Women's Club 151-155, 160, 269, 277
Pell, Claiborne 245
Pharr, John 248
Pitts, Hattie 250
Plummer, Bettie vi, ix, xi

Potomac and Ohio Railroad Depot (Washington, DC) 23-24
Public Interest Civic Association 155-158, 160, 196-197, 266
Pullman Company 131, 132, 133, 138-142, 143, 144, 184
Pullman Porters 101, 115-116, 130-132, 134, 220, 277
Randolph, A. Philip iii, iv, viii, 133-135, 136, 137, 138, 139, 143, 146, 147, 148, 149, 184-188, 202, 204, 207, 208, 218, 277-279
Pollard, Mary Ann Ruffin 2, 3, 4
Pride, James 156
Revells, Hiram 39
Riggs, Alice 52, 54
Riley, James Whitcomb 63
Robinson, William "Red" 41
Rockne, Knute 172
Roosevelt, Eleanor 185-186, 187, 189
Roosevelt, Franklin Delano 185, 186-187
Roosevelt, Theodore 66
Ruffin, Blanche Kemp 181
Ruffin, Eliza 5
Ruffin, Ellen 5
Ruffin, Henry "Harry" 1, 2-3, 245n
Ruffin, Henry, Jr. 2-3, 4, 5
Ruffin, Louis 2, 3, 4, 5-6
Ruffin, Mildred T. "Millie" 2, 3, 5, 6, 16, 52, 245n
Ruffin, Ottaway Francis vi
Ruffin, Robert D. 38
Ruffin, William 2, 3-4
Sands, Hazel 252
Saunders, Alice 258
Saunders, Helen 258
Saunders, James H. 258
Saunders, Jennie 258, 259
Savage, Frank 251
Second Baptist Church (Washington, DC) 36, 38, 44, 64-65, 80, 112, 113
Second Presbyterian Church (Westchester, PA) 84, 250

Shorter, Sadie 24
Slavery 1-2, 9-10, 11, 12-14, 21, 37, 57, 75, 134, 229, 230
Smalls, Robert 39
Smith, Ethel Robinson 169
Smith, Joseph 168-169
Sousa, John Philip 25
Spence, Anne Curry 95
Springfield College 167, 168, 171
Sunday, William Ashley "Billy" 85
Tabor Presbyterian Church 119-121
Taylor, Anderson 41
Taylor, Halley Blanton 121-125, 126, 138, 182, 200, 239, 281
Thompson, Caroline 8, 11-12, 52, 53, 219, 245n
Thompson, Henry 11, 52
Tillman, Benjamin R. "Pitchfork" 27
Totten, Ashley 135, 136, 149, 204
Tucker, Aaron 100, 101
Tucker, Berthea Johnson (second husband of Rosina Tucker) iv, v, 99-103, 104-106, 109, 130, 139-142, 168, 175-176, 178, 190, 192-193, 200, 201, 220-225, 260
Tucker, Claiborne 100n
Tucker, Fannie 100n
Tucker, Indiana "Indy" 100n, 102
Tucker, Lottie 100n
Tucker, Mary Johnson 100-101, 102, 103, 104, 106-107
Tucker, Minerva 100n
Tucker, Rosina Corrothers
    appearance i, 49-50, 246
    autobiography of ii-iii, vi
    with Brotherhood of Sleeping-Car Porters 115, 130, 135, 142, 143, 145-150, 190, 201, 202-204, 206-218, 254-255, 277
    childhood 17-25, 37-42
    church work 118-119, 125-129
    civic work 151-160, 189-191, 195-200, 266-272, 273-275

clerkship in U.S. Government 98
death 247-248
education of 15, 50-52
on feminism 229-230
funeral 248-249
health 94, 96-98, 225-226, 235, 245-247
illness and death of first husband (Corrothers) 87-88, 89-92
Ladies Auxiliary of Brotherhood of Sleeping-Car Porters, work with v, 115, 145-150, 190, 201, 202-204, 206-218, 254-255, 277
later years 225-229, 234-237, 245-247
marital discord (with Tucker) 104-106, 175-176
marries Corrothers 54-56
marries Tucker 102-103
musical training and activities   19-20, 22, 45-46, 47, 49, 70-71, 72, 75-77, 85, 106, 154, 256-257
personality vi
on race relations 232-233, 281-288
religious experiences and convictions 12, 36, 43-44, 45, 56-58, 92, 96, 98, 102, 159, 175-176, 180-181, 183, 193, 223, 224-225, 227-228, 237-41
in South Haven, Michigan 68-74
in U.S. Civil Defense Corps 160
Turner, Benjamin Sterling 39-40
Turner, Samuel 8
Virginia Union University 165, 166-167, 168, 171
Waldron, John Milton 110-111
Warfield, Mrs. Violet 127-128
Warfield, Miss Violet 128
Warfield, William Alonza 32
Warner, Glen S. "Pop" 172
Washington, DC
Daily life in 1890s 16-17, 24-25, 26-31, 48
Freedmen, conditions among 1-2
Race Relations 26-29
Race Riot of 1919 108-111

Webster, Milton Price 149, 207
White, Florence West 98-99
White, Walter Francis 160, 161
White, William 98-99
Wilberforce University 171, 192
Wilkinson, Garnet 50-51, 154
Willard, Frances 63
Williams, Charles 156
Wilson, Halena 148-149, 150, 203, 213
Wilson, Woodrow 27
Wormley, James 28n

www.ingramcontent.com/pod-product-compliance
Lightning Source LLC
Chambersburg PA
CBHW071957220426
43662CB00009B/1171